WEST BROMWICH ALBION

THE TOP 100 MATCHES

TONY MATTHEWS

FOREWORD BY
DEREK STATHAM

AMBERLEY

First published 2013

Amberley Publishing
The Hill, Stroud
Gloucestershire, GL5 4EP

www.amberleybooks.com

British Library Cataloguing in Publication Data.
A catalogue record for this book is available from the British Library.

ISBN 978 1 4456 1616 2 (print)
ISBN 978 1 4456 1631 5 (ebook)

Typeset in 10pt on 12pt Sabon.
Typesetting and Origination by Amberley Publishing.
Printed in the UK.

CONTENTS

FOREWORD BY DEREK STATHAM

I will never forget the day I made my League debut for Albion. It came in a 2-0 win at Stoke in December 1976 when I was just seventeen years old, and to celebrate the occasion I scored one of the goals.

That was some thirty-seven years ago. Even before I joined the club, the name West Bromwich Albion was well-known, certainly in Great Britain and even throughout Europe; although the club has only won the League Championship once – way back in 1920 – most of the teams, down the years, have produced some brilliant performances, and Tony has covered some of the finest in yet another splendid book.

I can readily recall some great games I played in during my twelve years at The Hawthorns, especially those against Manchester United, with the 4-0 win in 1977 and that terrific 5-3 victory at Old Trafford in 1978, which are firmly fixed in my mind.

I remember, also, the high-scoring games, with Coventry City (I actually scored in a 7-1 win) some exciting local derbies with rivals Aston Villa and Wolves; a few bruising yet exciting battles with Leeds United and Liverpool; several close contests with Tottenham Hotspur, Arsenal and Ipswich, as well as those tense and narrow matches against Manchester City and Nottingham Forest.

Wins, rather than defeats, tend to stand out in one's mind, and I'm sure that all ardent Baggies supporters will recall those I've mentioned above. But remember, League football has been in existence for 125 years, and since the outset in 1888, Albion, aided and abetted by some exceptionally fine players, have produced many record-breaking achievements, most of which are listed in the pages ahead.

During my professional career, I have played with and seen many of the game's finest footballers wearing the famous navy-blue-and-white striped shirts of West Bromwich Albion, such as record-breaking appearance-maker and goalscorer Tony Brown; the 'Three Degrees', namely Cyrille Regis, Laurie Cunningham and Brendon Batson; multi-talented midfielders Bryan Robson and Len Cantello; wing wizard Willie Johnston; two of the most dependable defenders ever, John Wile and Ally Robertson; strikers Bob Taylor, Andy Hunt, Don Goodman and Lee Hughes; plus five members of the foreign legion, Richard Sneekes, Thomas Gaardsoe, Zoltan Gera, Youssouf Mulumbu and Jonas Olsson. I must also mention some quality goalkeepers as well, including John Osborne, Tony Godden, Stuart Naylor, Russell Hoult and Ben Foster.

Way before my time, Albion won League games with class players in their ranks, the stars of yesteryear, including Billy Bassett, Tom Pearson, brothers Charlie and Tom Perry, brilliant full-back Jesse Pennington, father and son goalkeepers Hubert and Harold Pearson, 'wee' Tommy Magee,

Joe Carter, Jimmy Cookson, Teddy Sandford, Tommy Glidden, goal-machine 'W.G'. Richardson, Billy Elliott, the Irish duo of Dave Walsh and Jack Vernon, Len 'The Dependable' Millard, Ray Barlow, the 'Complete Footballer' himself Ronnie Allen, Bobby Robson, Derek Kevan, Jeff ' The King' Astle, Clive Clark, Don Howe, Joe Kennedy, Graham Williams, 'schemer-in-chief' Bobby Hope, John 'Yorky' Kaye and player-manager Johnny Giles.

Tony features all these, and many more, in his reports on Albion's best ever League wins.

Read and enjoy … and remember the good old days.

Derek Statham

INTRODUCTION

Question: How does one sit down and consider choosing Albion's best 100 wins in League football? It proved mighty difficult, I can tell you that, and I'm now 99 per cent certain that someone, somewhere, will contact me asking why I didn't include that win against Wolves, the away victory over Villa, triumphs over Liverpool, Everton and Manchester United and even a couple of Third Division successes?

After talking with the publishers, it was decided to cover precisely 100 victories, and the final decision was left to me as to what these would be, although I did get some guidance from a band of ardent supporters who between them confirmed at least seventy-five of the 'wins' covered in this book.

All I can say is that I wish I could have reported on, even mentioned, each and every one of Albion's 1,700+ victories they have so far achieved in the club's 125 years of League football since September 1888. It would have been a terrific publication if it were possible. Perhaps in the future it might just happen.

Goals, of course, win matches and I have elected to include a lot of Albion's high-scoring victories, along with the many close, drama-packed and nail-biting encounters. In fact, I have covered all of Albion's important wins, including those that clinched the championship, saved the team from relegation or secured promotion. I have also mentioned several victories achieved against local rivals, and those over high-ranking opponents at that time. Some exciting comebacks and a few shock results have also crept into text, plus many matches whereby a player stole the headlines with a hat-trick, a stunning goal, even a penalty or a last-gasp tap-in.

I have selected the semi-final and final of the 1993 play-offs in my top 100 wins, which technically were 'League' games. I know full well that every Baggies fan still enjoys reading about the 8-0 and 7-0 wins at Molineux and Villa Park in years gone by; thumping Manchester United 6-3 and 5-3 a decade apart; those eighteen goals Albion rammed past Birmingham City in three successive matches at St Andrew's; when Jimmy Cookson struck a club record six-timer in a Second Division victory over Blackpool; and finally when W. G. Richardson achieved the remarkable feat of scoring four goals in five minutes at West Ham.

I have also featured several matches in which an Albion player scored a hat-trick – and there are quite a few. I have covered the goalscoring ability, and for some, the creativity, of many of the club's star players, including Billy Bassett, Jasper Geddes, Tom Pearson, Fred Shinton and Fred Buck from the pre-WW1 era; Sid Bowser, Tommy Magee and Fred Morris from the 1920s; Tommy Glidden, Teddy Sandford and Joe Carter from the 1930s; Dave Walsh and Billy Elliott from the late 1940s; Ronnie Allen, Ray Barlow, Joe Kennedy, Frank Griffin, Derek Kevan and Bobby Robson from the 1950s; Jeff Astle, Tony Brown, Bobby Hope and company from the 1960s; Johnny Giles, Ally Brown, Bryan Robson, Cyrille Regis, Laurie Cunningham, Len Cantello, Derek Statham and their teammates from the 1970s; Gary Owen, Steve Mackenzie and Steve Hunt from the 1980s; Don Goodman, Bob Taylor, Andy Hunt, Ian Hamilton, Richard Sneekes, Paul Peschisolido and Bernard McNally from the 1990s; and, more recently, those of Lee Hughes, Kevin Phillips, Peter Odemwingie, Shane Long, Chris Brunt, James Morrison, Romelu Lukaku and others.

One cannot forget the work and commitment put in over the last 125 years by some terrific goalkeepers, by sturdy, resilient and highly competent defenders, by some of the game's finest and most skilful midfielders and wingers. In fact, a great save, a goal-line clearance, a last-ditch tackle, a lunging challenge, a defence-splitting pass, a corner, an innocuous cross, a penalty, a free-kick, has no doubt earned Albion an important victory, or two, somewhere down the line.

This book is all about 100 League games Albion have *won*, not lost or drawn. So let's now hope, and pray, they will add a few more to the list, which hopefully I can feature in a future publication covering the Baggies' greatest victories!

Tony Matthews

ACKNOWLEDGEMENTS

I would like to say a huge thank you, sincerely, to the many people who, over the years, have clarified, added to and corrected all my statistical information, club records, match reports and player profiles appertaining to West Bromwich Albion football club. And still, to this day, the odd few facts and/or statistics keep popping up which, if I've missed, one of these guys will pick up. Take a bow please, my 'best man' Colin Mackenzie and fellow fact-finders Robert Bradley and Steve Carr, who over the years have always come up with something extraordinary.

I also have to praise the following dedicated supporters who have provided me with photographs, cigarette and trade cards, caricature drawings and scrapbook cuttings for this, my latest book on the 'Baggies'... current club photographer Laurie Rampling, Neil Reynolds, Dean 'The Mask' Walton (Alumet Group), Dave Baxendale, Jonathan Eden, Peter Owen, Marc Soulsby, Paul Hammond, David Lister, Stuart Lees, Mick Greening, the late Warren Gwynne and lensman from the past Barry Marsh. Also, sincere thanks to go to Pat Bristoe of *doingthe92.co.uk* (if you want any cigarette cards *etc.* contact Pat); to opposing club supporters Paul Joannou, Nick Oldham, Mark Metcalf and Peter Hurn and, of course, to the handful of former players. Also, thanks to one of the club's greatest-ever left-backs, Derek Statham, for writing the foreword.

Special thanks, too, are afforded to Sarah Greenwood and Tom Furby and the rest of the staff at Amberley Publishing. Great job guys. And last but by no means least I must say 'thanks again' to my darling wife, Margaret, who never moans (really) when she sees me, head down, stuck in front of the computer, typing in word after word, with football books, magazines, newspaper cuttings and programmes scattered all around – mostly on the floor!

We've had arguments, everyone does, but she's there, backing me every inch of the way. Thanks love. I'll make up for lost time eventually, promise!

THE TOP 100 MATCHES

Flying Start
Stoke 0 Albion 2
Football League, 8 September 1888, Att. 4,524

This was Albion's first Football League game and victory over Stoke saw them top the table on goal average from Preston North End who, of course, went on to complete the double.

Fielding their strongest team, Albion – the FA Cup holders – created several chances in the first half but failed to make the vital breakthrough.

Continuing to have the majority of the play after the break, Albion were twice denied by Stoke's goalkeeper Billy Rowley, whose save from Tom Pearson was outstanding, while at the other end Albion's 'keeper Bob Roberts thwarted both Jimmy Sayer and Billy Tunnicliffe. It wasn't until ten minutes from time that the Baggies finally scored – and deservedly so. Stoke full-back Tommy Clare failed to control the ball under pressure. Albion's left-winger Joe Wilson dispossessed him and fired a shot straight between the posts from 15 yards to become the club's first-ever scorer in League football. Three minutes later, George Woodhall rose unchallenged to head in Billy Bassett's cross from the right to secure the points.

Around 1,500 Albion supporters saw this victorious team in action: Bob Roberts, Jack Horton, Harry Green, Ezra Horton, Charlie Perry, 'Jem' Bayliss, Billy Bassett, George Woodhall, Willie Hendrey, Tom Pearson and Joe Wilson.

Record Score
Albion 12 Darwen 0
League Division 1, 4 April 1892, Att. 1,109

With this win, Albion created Football League history by becoming the first team to score more than ten goals in a game and, in fact, 12-0 is still a record top-flight victory, although Nottingham Forest equalled it in 1909 when beating Leicester Fosse.

Albion, magnificent throughout, struck first after ninety seconds. Willie Groves found left-winger Jasper Geddes and his low cross was thumped high into the net by Pearson. Keeping goal for Darwen was Billy McOwen who, four and a half years earlier, had conceded half a dozen goals when Albion lost 7-6 in a friendly at Blackburn.

After Bassett had hit the bar and both Pearson and Sammy Nicholls had shot over, Groves saw an effort disallowed before Jack Reynolds put Albion two up by heading in Jasper Geddes'

Above left: George Woodhall, who scored Albion's second game in their first-ever League game at Stoke on 8 September 1888.

Above right: Billy Bassett was Albion's four-goal hero in the record win over Darwen, and also star of the fight-back against Nottingham Forest.

left-wing corner on twenty minutes. Bassett bagged a third after a mazy dribble in the twenty-ninth minute; Reynolds diverted Geddes' free-kick home for number four seven minutes later and on the stroke of half-time, Pearson made it five after excellent work, initially by goalkeeper Joe Reader for a smart throw out and then by Bassett.

In fact, Reader, apart from handling a couple of looping crosses, did not have a single shot to save in the first forty-five minutes, spending most of the time leaning against an upright!

Darwen had nothing to offer, and after Pearson and Geddes had gone close to increasing Albion's goal tally, Bassett obliged with two more in the forty-eighth and fifty-second minutes to complete his hat-trick: the first from a scramble 10 yards from the goal-line, his second a well-struck free-kick from 20 yards after Pearson had been fouled.

After a relatively quiet period when Albion managed only three shots, Pearson headed goal number eight on seventy-three minutes from Bassett's cross. This was followed soon afterwards by an unfortunate own-goal conceded by right-back Ted Hunt, before the impressive Pearson took Albion into double figures after dribbling past four opponents. At this juncture, Albion had equalled the League scoring record of 10-0, set by Preston against Stoke three years earlier. Their next target was to score twice more, without conceding, to establish a new League record for the biggest win, which at the time was held by Aston Villa who had defeated Accrington 12-2 just three weeks earlier.

And that record was duly achieved – but only just, when Geddes darted in to head home number eleven in the eighty-fifth minute and the hard-working Nicholls put both the ball and goalkeeper McOwen in the back of the net with just seconds remaining.

It was a pity that such a small band of supporters turned out to see this record-breaking victory. Anticipating another goal rush, 10,000 fans attended Albion's next home game against Stoke, which ended in a 2-2 draw. And surprisingly, the return fixture with Darwen, played on 16 April, also finished level!

The nearest any Albion team has come to scoring a dozen goals in a competitive match since this one-sided win over the Lancashire cotton town team was a 9-2 First Division victory over Manchester City in 1957.

Great Fight Back
Nottingham Forest 3 Albion 4
League Division 1, 2 March 1893, Att. 4,100

This was the first time Albion had played on a Thursday other than over Christmas, and after half an hour they wished they hadn't bothered turning up as Forest were leading 3-0 and strolling!

With a strong wind behind them, the hosts scored after six minutes, Jock McCallum firing past Reader from 10 yards. Soon afterwards, the Albion 'keeper clearly 'kicked' Horace Pike off the ball when he was preparing to 'score', but the referee waved play on. Following two superb saves by Reader, Forest bagged a second goal on twenty-one minutes when Harry Daft scored from a corner. Soon afterwards, Albion's right-half Tom Perry handled inside the box and John McPherson comfortably netted the penalty.

Looking dead and buried, Albion pulled a goal back on thirty-four minutes when Bassett poked in Jasper Geddes' low cross and, with their tails up, the Baggies struck again on the stroke of half-time, Geddes scoring after Bassett's shot had been saved.

Albion began the second half with all guns blazing and in the forty-ninth minute Bassett equalised from Pearson's pass. Daft then missed an easy chance for Forest before Albion came again, and after Geddes and Pearson had gone close, left-half Willie Groves drove in the winning goal to complete a remarkable comeback.

Christmas Socking for Wolves!
Wolverhampton Wanderers 0 Albion 8
League Division 1, 27 December 1893, Att. 8,000

This Black Country derby turned out to be a non-event as Albion virtually dictated play from the first to the last whistle.

The visitors got off to a flying start against the FA Cup holders, Roddy McLeod tapping home from 8 yards after just fifty-five seconds. Wolves threatened briefly, Alf Griffin having a goal disallowed for offside, and Harry Wood seeing his shot saved by Albion's 'keeper Reader. But back came Albion, and after Geddes had hit a post, centre-half Charlie Perry ventured upfield to make it 2-0 with a powerful header from Bassett's corner on sixteen minutes.

Eight minutes later, Bassett cut inside full-back George Swift to score number three; McLeod pounced on an error by Tommy Dunn to tuck away Albion's fourth goal after half an hour, and

Above left: Tom Pearson, Albion's leading goalscorer from 1888 to 1893.

Above right: Roddy McLeod was too hot to handle at Molineux in 1895.

Below left: A caricature drawing of Tom Perry, who scored Albion's sixth goal in their end-of-season victory over Sheffield Wednesday on 22 April 1895.

the same player was unlucky soon afterwards when his shot was deflected onto a post by Hill Griffiths.

Albion continued to press forward and just before half-time, Bassett, unmarked inside the penalty area, smashed home Geddes' pinpoint pass to make it 5-0. After future Albion player Joe Butcher had struck the bar in a rare Wolves attack, McLeod scored his hat-trick goal from Bassett's pass on sixty-two minutes.

This was the Scot's second treble for Albion – his first came in a 7-1 home League win over Burnley eleven months earlier.

Owen Williams, deputising for Pearson, found room to score number seven in the seventy-first minute, although Wolves goalkeeper Crispin Rose should have saved the inside-left's weak effort. Six minutes from time, Bassett completed his hat-trick with a 15-yard volley from Williams' 10-yard pass.

This emphatic 8-0 victory remains as Albion's best away from home in League football, while for Wolves it is their heaviest home defeat ever in all competitions.

The local *Express & Star* journalist wrote, 'Wolves were simply wretched, with the exception of Owen. Albion simply made rings around the Wanderers. I've never seen the cup holders so completely hopelessly beaten.'

It would be more than forty-two years before two Albion players would each score a hat-trick in the same League game, Jack Mahon and W. G. Richardson obliging in an 8-1 win over Blackburn in 1936.

Win Target Achieved in Style
Albion 6 Sheffield Wednesday 0
League Division 1, 22 April 1895, Att. 8,217

Two days after the disappointment of losing 1-0 to Aston Villa in the FA Cup final, Albion knew they *had* to win their final League game of the season against Wednesday by at least *five* clear goals to avoid competing in the test matches, which ultimately could result in relegation to the Second Division.

Stoke (twenty-four points), Derby County (twenty-three) and Liverpool (twenty-two) were sitting above Albion in thirteenth, fourteenth and fifteenth positions, and all three had completed their League programme. So it was imperative that Albion won and won well!

In fact, they not only beat Wednesday, they slaughtered them to the tune of 6-0. With the wind behind them and kicking down the famous Stoney Lane slope, an excited crowd saw left-winger Geddes, re-signed from Millwall for the last three games of the season, open the scoring with a header from Bassett's cross after just fifty seconds.

Fifteen minutes later. Tommy Green, making only his fourth appearance of the season, nodded home number two, reacting quickest after Bassett's shot had been saved by 'keeper Bill Allan.

Knowing that if the Owls scored it could prove disastrous, Albion continued on the offensive. Full-back Billy Williams had a 25-yard indirect free-kick disallowed, McLeod and Green both struck the woodwork and Geddes fired over. Thankfully, the latter quickly made amends by nodding home Bassett's superb cross on thirty-five minutes.

Then, with the referee poised to blow for half-time and with visitor's defence all at sea, Albion's five-goal target became realistically possible when Tom Hutchinson drove in a fourth goal, after some fine approach play by Bassett and Geddes.

Albion powered on after the break. McLeod duly added a fifth goal, netting through a ruck of players following Jack Taggart's short free-kick, and having seen 'keeper Reader and his co-defenders block out the Owls, Tom Perry's shot went in off the angle to make it 6-0 with fifteen minutes remaining. There were celebrations aplenty after this famous victory.

Albion certainly won in style and the *Midland Chronicle* reporter stated, 'The Albion has never given a finer display in the history of the club – had Geddes been on the left wing on Saturday [in the cup final] Albion would have won.'

Albion finished fourth from bottom of the table on twenty-four points, leaving Liverpool to contest the dreaded test matches, the equivalent of today's play-offs.

First Hawthorns Win

Albion 3 Manchester City 2
League Division 1, 6 October 1900, Att. 11,183

This was Albion's first win at The Hawthorns.

Black Country born centre-half Abe Jones got the Baggies off to a flying start, netting in the fourth minute with a header from Ben Garfield's cross.

However, five minutes later, with Albion on top, City were handed an equaliser when Baggies' 'keeper Reader, under pressure from Billy Meredith, conceded an own-goal. Meredith then had the ball in the net again but the referee disallowed the goal, indicating that the Welshman had fouled Jones, who had in fact had tripped Meredith!

Halfway through the first half Billy Richards, replacing the injured Chippy Simmons for his only start of the season, and his last-ever game for the club, restored Albion's lead from John Chadburn's cross.

Former England international Fred Wheldon went close to increasing Albion's lead before Garfield struck in the sixtieth minute to make it 3-1. Soon afterwards the same player fired into the side-netting and Chadburn shot wide from 10 yards. Then, out of the blue, Billy Holmes, completely unmarked inside the penalty area, bagged a second for the visitors to make it a nervous last twenty minutes for the Baggies, who were mighty relieved when City had two goals disallowed, although at the other end of the field, Richards (twice) and Garfield bought excellent saves out of City's goalkeeper Charlie Williams.

Unfortunately, Albion lost the return fixture in Manchester 1-0 as they battled, in vain, to stay in the First Division.

Star Buck

Albion 7 Bolton Wanderers 2
League Division 1, 8 December 1900, Att. 8,157

Dick Roberts became the first Albion player to score a hat-trick at The Hawthorns, doing so in this resounding 7-2 win over Bolton Wanderers.

Having lost 4-0 at Derby the week before, wholesale changes were made by the selection committee. Reader returned in goal after injury, replacing Joe Lowe, while left-back Amos Dunn and forwards Chadburn and Simmons were all axed in favour of George Cave, Fred Buck and Garfield.

Buck, signed from Stafford Rangers, was making his debut and partnered Roberts on the right-wing. He had a terrific game, with the *Free Press* reporter stating, 'Not since (Billy) Bassett was first introduced into the Albion front rank, has any player in that department of the team signalled his first appearance with a cleverer and sounder exhibition that Buck did.'

Bolton went ahead on seven minutes when Bill Tracey scored against the run of play. Albion hit back immediately and after Buck had a 'goal' disallowed for offside, right-half Jack Banks cracked in the equaliser from Roberts' corner. In Albion's next attack, Roberts struck the first of his three goals to put his side ahead.

Wheldon, from Buck's astute pass, and Garfield with a crisp, low drive, added further goals to send Albion in at half-time with a commanding 4-1 lead.

Although Jim McKie reduced the deficit in the sixtieth minute, Albion were always in control and after Garfield, centre-forward Jim Stevenson and Wheldon had gone close, Buck celebrated his first game with Albion's fifth goal on seventy-two minutes. Roberts then went on to complete his hat-trick in the seventy-fifth and seventy-ninth minutes to seal an excellent victory.

Unfortunately, despite this superb win, Albion lost their next three games and won only three of their remaining seven matches to finish bottom of the table and so suffer relegation for the first time in the club's history.

Run Extended

Albion 7 Blackpool 2
League Division 2, 22 February 1902, Att. 6,249

On a miserable afternoon, on a heavy, cloggy pitch, Albion extended their unbeaten home run to twelve games with this easy victory over the Seasiders.

A goal down to Geordie Anderson's strike on ten minutes, full-back Jack Kifford equalised straight away with a booming free-kick. Ex-Wolves player Tom Worton then made it 2-1 and on the half-hour mark, Stevenson scored a third to put Albion firmly in control.

In the thirty-fourth minute, Worton netted his second of the game to make it 4-1, Simmons banged in a fifth eight minutes later and just before the break, the same player slotted home number six. Albion were rampant, Blackpool demoralised.

The visitors, though, hit back and Anderson reduced the arrears early in the second half, only for Simmons to complete the rout with his hat-trick goal on sixty-three minutes.

Late on, Simmons, Worton and Jimmy McLean all had chances to increase Albion's lead while at the other end of the field, and goalkeeper Ike Webb saved well from Anderson as Blackpool battled to the bitter end.

Simmons' hat-trick was the first by an Albion player in a Second Division match at The Hawthorns, and two weeks later Worton followed with a treble in a 4-0 win over Newton Heath (now Manchester United) as Albion roared on towards the championship.

High-Flying Magpies Blitzed

Albion 6 Newcastle United 1
League Division 1, 27 September 1902, Att. 22,160

After three straight wins, high-flying Newcastle were brought crashing down to earth by promoted Albion, who produced a brilliant exhibition of attacking football.

Billy Lee put the Baggies ahead on three minutes after United's goalkeeper Matt Kingsley had failed to clear his lines. Buck made it 2-0 fifteen minutes later after some excellent work by

An action picture of Charlie 'Chippy' Simmons, who scored a hat-trick against the Seasiders, 1902.

Harry Hadley and McLean and, with the visitors under pressure, George Dorsett swung over a corner, Kingsley flapped at, and missed, the high ball and, as it dropped, Simmons tucked in number three.

Shortly before the break, Bob McColl pulled a goal back for the visitors when Dan Nurse was caught in possession, but after that it was all Albion who scored three more goals as they commanded the second half.

Buck raced clear to fire in number four from the edge of the area on forty-nine minutes. Stevenson banged home a 35-yard piledriver with twenty minutes remaining and after Baggies' full-back Kifford had missed a penalty, McLean's right-footer six minutes from time sealed Newcastle's fate. Albion were now third in the table, a point behind leaders Notts County, and this excellent result was reported as a 'huge shock' in the footballing press.

No Return For Rovers
Albion 5 Blackburn Rovers 3
League Division 1, 22 November 1902, Att. 12,134

Albion made it six League wins on the bounce with this hard-earned, but deserved, victory over an efficient Rovers side.

With forwards Buck and Dorsett out through injury, McLean and Andrew 'Scottie' Smith came back into the team, and both did very well, being involved in the action time and again.

The first half produced five goals – and there could, and should, have been more!

McLean and Simmons combined to set up Billy Lee, who fired the Baggies in front on six minutes. Although Hugh Morgan equalised sixty seconds later, Simmons restored Albion's lead in the twenty-first minute with a header from Worton's superb cross.

Rovers inside-right Jimmy Robertson then raced between Dan Nurse and Hadley to make it 2-2 and just before the interval, Arnie Whittaker netted again for the visitors as Baggies centre-half Stevenson stood rooted to the spot!

Unfortunately, early in the second half, Rovers lost Robertson through injury and also had Billy Bow limping on the left wing. From this point on, Albion took complete control.

On fifty-one minutes, Smith flicked on for Simmons who was tripped inside the box by Bob Crompton. Kifford's penalty struck the crossbar, resulting in a desperate goalmouth scrimmage which ended with Kifford's making amends by sending the ball flying into the roof of the net.

Then, with twenty minutes remaining, Smith picked out Stevenson, who raced forward to make it 4-3 and almost immediately Worton smacked home McLean's cross for Albion's fifth goal. In the last five minutes, Rovers were unlucky when Whittaker hit a post, while at the other end Worton had a 'goal' disallowed and Lee was foiled by 'keeper Joyce with the goal at his mercy.

This was Albion's fourteenth home League game against Rovers and they had only lost one of the previous thirteen, a 2-1 defeat in December 1892.

Bantams Cooked!
Albion 6 Bradford City 1
League Division 2, 11 November 1905, Att. 9,000

Albion, unchanged for the fifth successive game, got off to a flying start, scoring twice through centre-forward Fred Shinton and inside-left Adam Haywood in the opening ten minutes, with the visitors' defence at sixes and sevens!

Although Andy McGeachan replied for City from a corner halfway through the first half when Arthur Randle and Ted Pheasant stood watching each other, Shinton struck again to give Albion a 3-1 interval lead.

Simmons added a fourth goal early in the second half, after smart work by right-winger Herbert Varney and Haywood, and with acres of space in which to work after City had been reduced to nine men following the departure of Fred Halliday (injured) and Jimmy Conlin (sent off) Albion drove forward in numbers.

Shinton, set up by outside-left Ernie Perkins, completed his hat-trick with a fine drive from 20 yards, and Simmons grabbed a sixth goal with a clinical finish after some clever interplay between Varney and right-half Sammy Peters.

With City struggling, Shinton, Haywood and Perkins should have added to Albion's goal tally, but in the end the home fans went home happy! An Albion team has never since scored six goals in a League game against the Bradford, the next best victory being 4-1 in 1919.

Four-Goal Shinton
Albion 6 Grimsby Town 1
League Division 2, 25 December 1906, Att.19,047

Watched by a good-sized holiday crowd, Albion's robust centre-forward Shinton celebrated Christmas in style with his third four-timer of the season. He was certainly bang in form, having netted twenty League goals in the first half of the campaign, including fours against Clapton Orient and Glossop and a hat-trick versus Gainsborough Trinity.

A caricature drawing of Fred Shinton, who netted twenty-eight League goals for Albion in 1906/07, including a four-timer in a 6-1 win over Grimsby Town on Christmas Day 1906.

After three near misses, Albion took the lead in fifteen minutes when Tommy Dilly, cutting in from the left, scored with a fine low shot.

Two minutes later, Haywood added a second with another smart finish, and halfway through the first half, after Dilly had struck a post, Shinton bagged his first goal to make it 3-0. Although Alf Robinson pulled a goal back for the visitors, against the run of play, Albion moved forward in menacing fashion. Shinton got up some extra steam and powered in three more goals between the fiftieth and sixty-second minutes as the visitors' defence crumbled under pressure.

Late on, Shinton uncharacteristically missed two easy chances; Dilly again hit an upright, while Haywood and wing-half Arthur Randle had shots saved by Grimsby's over-worked reserve goalkeeper Jim Horner.

Shinton ended 1906/07 with a club record twenty-eight League goals to his credit, despite missing eight games through injury from late January. This record would stand until 1920 when Fred Morris took over the mantle with a tally of thirty-seven.

Limp Imps
Albion 5 Lincoln City 2
League Division 2, 21 December 1907, Att. 7,000

Five goals were scored in the last quarter of an hour of this highly entertaining pre-Christmas encounter at The Hawthorns.

This was Albion's ninth League meeting with the Imps and victory was the biggest of the five recorded so far.

After Buck, the Reverend Billy Jordan and David Walker had all missed chances for Albion, Billy Langham surprisingly put the Imps ahead after twenty-five minutes. Shaken but not stirred, Albion responded and, after Jordan, Sammy Timmins and right-winger George Garratt had squirmed easy chances, Buck equalised with a penalty shortly before half-time.

Play was frantic at the start of the second half and both goalkeepers were kept busy, Albion's Jimmy Stringer twice saving low down from Langham.

After several close shaves and horrible misses at both ends, all of a sudden the goals rained in thick and fast.

David Walker and Jordan scored for Albion in the seventy-seventh and seventy-ninth minutes to make it 3-1; Buck then missed a second penalty before Langham scored again for the visitors, only for Albion to receive a third spot-kick, which was put away this time by the cool-headed Walker. Inside-right Fred Wilcox rounded things off with Albion's fifth goal on eighty-eight minutes.

This was Albion's second-biggest win of the season.

Mariners All at Sea

Albion 7 Grimsby Town 0
League Division 2, 2 January 1909, Att. 5,177

A disappointing crowd saw Albion extend their unbeaten run to thirteen matches with this emphatic win over the Mariners. Backed by a strong wind and kicking towards the Birmingham Road end, Albion took the lead on two minutes through debutant inside-left Sid Bowser, who added a second from ex-Aston Villa forward Billy Garraty's shrewd pass thirteen minutes later.

Buck, still chief penalty-taker, then missed again from the spot before Garraty swept home Albion's third goal ten minutes from half-time.

In the second half it was all Albion. Buck (forty-eight minutes), Jack Manners with a terrific 25-yard drive (on seventy-two), Garraty (in the seventy-third) and right-winger Willie Thompson (on eighty-eight) scored further goals to give the Baggies a resounding victory.

For the record, Grimsby had just three shots at goal to Albion's twenty. The visitors' woodwork was also struck twice.

This was Albion's sixth home game against Grimsby in seven years and after this latest win, their goal tally stood at an impressive seventeen. In the next seven home games against the Mariners, the Baggies would net another twenty-five goals, making it forty-two in thirteen starts.

Billy Garraty hit two goals in Albion's 7-0 win over Grimsby in January 1909.

Promoted as Champions
Albion 1 Huddersfield Town 0
League Division 2, 29 April 1911, Att. 30,135

This single-goal victory clinched the Second Division championship for Albion and The Hawthorns' biggest crowd of the season saw them do it.

Going into this final match, Albion could have got away with a draw, but they didn't know that at the time, and were fully committed against a resilient Huddersfield side.

At the time of kick-off, Albion were leading the table on fifty-one points; Chelsea and Bolton Wanderers, each with two games to play, were lying second and third on forty-nine points apiece.

Looking apprehensive at times, Albion came close early on when Bowser, leading the attack in place of the injured Bob Pailor, saw his header saved by Welsh international goalkeeper Richmond Roose, and soon afterwards left-winger Amos Lloyd fired low across the visitors' 6-yard box with Bowser unable to get a touch.

The visitors were putting in some hefty challenges and, in the twenty-sixth minute, Fred Bullock clumsily bundled over Willie Thompson as he raced into the box. It was a blatant penalty and up stepped inside-left Buck to drive his kick straight through the legs of Roose. Lucky, yes, but the ball was in the net! It was Buck's tenth and most important goal of the season, without doubt!

Albion dictated the reminder of the half with Lloyd causing plenty of problems, along with Bowser and Harry Wright.

Things changed after the break as the visitors pressed forward, but despite being under the cosh for long periods, Albion's defence, with full-backs Joe Smith and Jesse Pennington outstanding, stood firm, while goalkeeper Hubert Pearson pulled off several fine saves, one from Joe Jee being first-class. It was tense but Albion survived, and so clinched the Second Division title to regain their top-flight status.

As it was Albion finished two points clear of Bolton (53-51) and four ahead of Chelsea.

A First for Bowser
Albion 4 Bradford City 1
League Division 1, 27 September 1919, Att. 29,680

The first defender ever to score a hat-trick in a competitive game for Albion was Bowser, who achieved the feat in this tough encounter at The Hawthorns.

Having returned to the club in 1914, Handsworth-born Bowser was now Albion's centre-half, having previously been a goalscoring inside-left, and in this game he certainly knew how to blast the ball between the posts!

Albion, beginning slowly, grabbed the lead with a fifth-minute penalty when City's right-back Craig Brown handled Claude Jephcott's right-wing cross. Bowser smashed the spot-kick past Jock Ewart.

Albion continued to dominate, but it was City who scored next, Jimmy Marshall equalising on the counter-attack with a rising shot on thirty-three minutes.

After that, Albion buckled down to business. Jack Crisp missed Jephcott's cross by inches, Ewart saved from Morris and Jephcott fired wide.

Above left: Tommy Magee, seen here in his England kit, scored Albion's last goal in the 8-0 win over Notts County in October 1919.

Above right: Programme front: WBA *v.* Huddersfield Town, 29 April 1911.

Below left: Sid Bowser, Albion's penalty expert.

Right: Sid Bowser head-and-shoulders shot.

The lead was restored on fifty-five minutes when Bowser scored his second goal, this time with a booming free-kick from 20 yards after Andy Smith had been fouled on the edge of the area by Joe Hargreaves.

Thwarted thereafter by Ewart, who saved well from Tommy Magee and Jephcott, the Bradford 'keeper was left helpless when Morris added a third goal in the sixty-second minute after a left-wing move between McNeal and Crisp.

Eight minutes later Morris, lining himself up to score again, was bundled over by Ernie Storer and Nottingham referee Arthur Watson had no hesitation in awarding Albion another penalty.

As before, Bowser cracked home the spot-kick to complete his hat-trick and so write himself into the record books. In fact, three minutes from time, Albion should have had a third penalty, when Ewart bowled over both Morris and Crisp as they chased a long ball into the area.

It would be another forty-five years before another Albion defender would score a hat-trick in a League game – and that was right-back Bobby Cram in a 5-3 victory over Stoke City in 1964.

Magical Morris
Albion 8 Notts County 0
League Division 1, 25 October 1919, Att. 36,086

This resounding victory was Albion's biggest of the twenty-eight they achieved in their only League championship-winning season to date.

With four key players missing – goalkeeper Pearson, Smith, Bowser and Jephcott – Albion still dominated proceedings from the start, and in fact, reserve 'keeper Len Moorwood was hardly troubled during the entire ninety minutes, having only two direct shots to deal with, from Harry Hill on twenty-seven minutes and from Billy McLeod late on.

Morris was Albion's 'star of the show'. He scored five goals, his first as early as the fifth minute when, after some intricate play involving Magee, Andy Smith and McNeal, he was on the spot to blast Crisp's cross past 'keeper Albert Iremonger.

Hotshot Morris then made it 2-0 with a brilliant solo effort on forty minutes, and six minutes into the second half, he completed his hat-trick with a low right-foot shot from Magee's angled pass.

Unfortunately, County's overworked right-back Jack Foster turned another Crisp centre into his own net to make it 4-0 in the sixty-first minute, and soon afterwards the already beleaguered visitors were reduced to ten men when Horace Henshaw hobbled off following a tackle by Sammy Richardson.

After the unstoppable Morris had fired in two more goals in the seventieth and seventy-second minutes – the first created by Magee, the second from Crisp's pass – a wonderful dummy by Smith allowed outside-left Howard Gregory to sneak in for a seventh goal with eleven minutes remaining, before Magee rounded things off with an eighth goal five minutes from time.

Amazingly, a week later Albion travelled to Meadow Lane for the return fixture and lost 2-0! Work that one out.

To this day, 8-0 remains as Albion's best-ever victory over County, and it's also the Baggies' joint second-biggest League win in terms of goal difference, behind their 12-0 drubbing of Darwen in 1892.

And by going nap, Morris became the first player to score five times in a top-flight League game or major cup tie for the club. Only one other player has achieved this feat since – Derek Kevan against Everton in 1960. Jimmy Cookson would score six goals (a double hat-trick) in a Second Division match *v.* Blackpool in 1927.

Foe Well Beaten
Aston Villa 2 Albion 4
League Division 1, 15 November 1919, Att. 58,273

This, the fortieth local League derby between the clubs, 'was well contested throughout', wrote the editor of the *Athletic News*, who added, 'Albion's victory was due in the main to the resolution and accuracy of Gregory and Morris. Each held the ball and drew the defence and rarely erred in their marksmanship. I doubt if there is a more solid, scheming, cleverer inside-left than Morris. He is half the attack.'

Albion, beaten 2-1 at home by Villa five days earlier, were keen on revenge and early on both Morris and Crisp (replacing the injured Magee) saw shots saved by goalkeeper Sam Hardy, while at the other end, Pearson dealt comfortably with efforts from Billy Kirton and Charlie Wallace.

After pushing Albion back, Villa took the lead on twenty-two minutes when Kirton scored from Clem Stephenson's square pass.

Six minutes later, Albion drew level when Morris ran between Frank Barson and Jimmy Harrop to set up Gregory who netted from 10 yards.

There was plenty of endeavour after this but no real goal threat, Albion coming closest to scoring when Morris fired over from 15 yards.

In the fiftieth minute, Albion took the lead. Jephcott raced past full-back Tommy Weston before delivering the perfect cross for Morris, who scored with ease.

After Villa defender Jack Thompson had cleared another Morris effort off the line, Gregory dashed away, dragged Hardy out of position, and slipped in Morris for another comfortable

Claude Jephcott, in great form at Villa Park, 1919.

goal. Three minutes later it was 4-1 when Hardy fumbled Crisp's low shot, allowing Gregory to poke home from 6 yards.

As the snow began to fall, Albion continued to attack and should have increased their lead through Jephcott and Morris, the latter failing in a one-on-one situation.

Villa rallied late on and Walter Boyman reduced the deficit on eighty minutes.

This was a fine win for Albion – their fifth in eight visits to Villa Park since 1900.

Champs End on High

Albion 4 Chelsea 0
League Division 1, 1 May 1920, Att. 35,668

The attendance for Albion's last game of their championship-winning season was 5,000 above the average. Before the kick-off, club chairman and former player Mr William Bassett hoisted the Football League flag while the town's band played 'Conquering Hero' as skipper Pennington led out the team.

Having scored only once in their previous three games, Albion wanted to end on a high and they did just that, thumping third-placed Chelsea 4-0!

Unfortunately, Morris, with thirty-seven goals to his name and needing one more to equal the record set by Everton's Bert Freeman in 1908/09 for most scored in the top flight, was desperately unlucky throughout and failed to find the net. He had at last half a dozen chances as his teammates regularly fed him with passes. But unfortunately he missed the target, whereas his colleagues hit it!

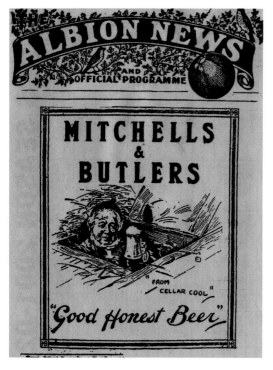

Programme front: WBA *v.* Chelsea (4-0), 1 May 1920, the last game of the championship-winning season.

Chelsea hardly threatened, mustering just three shots at goal in ninety minutes as Albion ran the show from the start. In fact, they should have taken the lead in the third minute, but Morris fired wide, as did Crisp soon afterwards.

The breakthrough finally arrived on seventeen minutes when McNeal, steaming forward, thumped home a cracker high into the net from near the penalty spot after Chelsea's centre-half Tom Logan had blocked an effort from Andy Smith.

Although in control, Albion didn't add to their goal tally until the forty-sixth minute, when left-winger Gregory's looping header from Crisp's cross crept over the line as the Chelsea 'keeper Jimmy Molyneux lost his footing.

Smith's 15-yard drive on fifty minutes made it 3-0 and Bentley, with a close range shot from Crisp's centre, netted a fourth just before the hour. To his credit, Morris assisted in two of the goals and never stopped working.

At the final whistle, hundreds of fans raced onto the pitch and congregated in front of the director's box to see the First Division trophy presented to left-back Pennington by the Football League president John McKenna who said in his speech, 'never has the championship been won by a more brilliant team'.

In 1919/20, Albion set three records by scoring 104 goals, winning twenty-eight matches and amassing sixty points. Sheffield Wednesday would break the scoring record with 105 in 1929/30; Spurs eventually claimed more wins, thirty-one in 1960/61, and although equalled by Liverpool in 1921/22 and Sheffield Wednesday in 1929/30, Albion's tally of sixty points would remain a record until Arsenal gained sixty-six in 1930/31.

A fortnight after their final League game, Albion defeated Tottenham Hotspur 2-0 at White Hart Lane to lift the FA Charity Shield.

Arsenal 'Gunned' Down
Albion 7 Arsenal 0
League Division 1, 14 October 1922, Att. 21,730

Albion, beaten 3-1 at Highbury seven days earlier, turned the tables on the Gunners with a solid and efficient performance.

Ivor Jones headed wide in Albion's first attack and Clem Voysey grazed a post as the Gunners responded. Soon afterwards Jones (again) and Morris both tested Stephen Dunn, in the Arsenal goal, but the visitors had come with a plan – to try and catch Albion's two wingers, Crisp and Gregory offside. It backfired!

The Gunners at times looked threatening going forward and, in fact, were in the middle of a decent spell when, slightly against the run of play, Albion took the lead in the twenty-ninth minute through Morris, who netted from close range after 'keeper Dunn had mishandled Stan Davies' shot.

Three minutes later, with right-back Frank Bradshaw exposed, Gregory and Morris broke down the left and as Bobby Turnbull slipped, Morris pounced and found the net with a low shot from 10 yards.

Davies thought he had scored on thirty-eight minutes, but his effort was ruled out for handball and just before half-time, Arsenal's Harry White went close with a header.

Although trailing by two, the visitors persisted with their offside tactics and fussy referee Jack Bunnell riled the home fans with his petty whistle blowing.

Albion picked up their game and steadily drove Arsenal back. Crisp fired over, Alf Baker somehow scrambled Davies's shot off the line and Dunn denied Morris.

Then the floodgates opened. Arsenal simply collapsed, conceding five goals in less than a quarter of an hour.

Davies triggered things off in the seventy-first minute, driving the ball across the penalty area for Crisp to clip home. Five minutes later, Gregory's shot rebounded off a post to Jones whose deft touch enabled Morris to complete his hat-trick.

Fifty seconds later Crisp, unmarked, stroked home a loose ball to make it 5-0; Gregory fired in Morris's pass for number six on seventy-seven minutes and after Davies had shaved a post, Morris walked in his fourth goal and Albion's seventh goal with six minutes remaining.

This remains as Albion's biggest-ever win over the Gunners.

Visitors 'Hammered'

Albion 7 West Ham United 1
League Division 1, 24 October 1925, Att. 20,851

Having won only four of their previous fourteen League games, Albion hit top form by literally 'hammering' the Londoners in this rather one-sided contest.

With a strong wind behind them, the Baggies started well, Charlie 'Tug' Wilson having two low shots saved by goalkeeper Ted Hufton. After one penalty appeal was turned down when Tommy Hodgson clearly handled, the Baggies' were successful with a second claim on twenty-two minutes as Albert Cadwell put hand to ball. Davies stepped up only to thump his spot-kick against a post, but luckily the ball bounced down, hit the right foot of Hufton and spun back over the line. An own-goal? 'No way,' said Davies, 'it's mine'.

Six minutes later, a great pass by Joe Carter sent Tommy Glidden away down the right. The winger cut inside Hodgson and scored with a terrific cross shot.

As the rain came down, the visitors hit back and Dicky Baugh cleared Jimmy Ruffell's shot off the line, but then it was about-turn as West Ham's defence was penetrated again, ninety seconds before the interval, as Davies turned in Glidden's right-wing centre for number three.

Joe Carter netted twice against the Hammers
(Albion 7 West Ham 1), 24 October 1925.

The visitors were stunned and, seven minutes after the break, in dazzling sunshine, Wilson stabbed in a fourth goal for Albion after some clever work by Carter.

After Ruffell had shaved the bar in a rare Hammers' attack, Glidden did likewise for Albion who subsequently increased their lead on sixty-four minutes when Carter broke through to net his first goal of the season.

There was some joy for the Hammers when Ruffell netted a seventy-third-minute penalty, after Baugh's unfortunate handball. This 'goal' was similar to Davies' early spot-kick as the ball hit Albion's 'keeper George Ashmore before rebounding into the net off a post.

Six minutes later, Davies collected Bill Richardson's long pass, charged the through the middle and completed his hat-trick and, to round things off, Carter made it 'seventh heaven' in the eighty-first minute from Glidden's pass.

West Ham, beaten FA Cup finalists two years earlier, simply couldn't match Albion for skill and commitment, and this emphatic victory remains, to this day, as the Baggies' biggest over the Hammers in competitive football.

Six of the Best

Albion 6 Aston Villa 2
League Division 1, 12 March 1927, Att. 50,392

Albion, fighting against relegation, dominated the first half of this West Midlands encounter. However, they had only one goal to show for their efforts – a twenty-first-minute strike from Glidden following a darting run by winger Jack Byers and a clever pass from Sammy Short who was playing in his first local derby.

Prior to that, Welsh schemer Ivor Jones had the ball in net but was flagged offside while both Davies and Short saw shots saved by Villa's goalkeeper Tommy Jackson.

When the visitors did venture forward they certainly looked dangerous. Clem Stephenson went close with a 15-yard grub-hunter and burly centre-forward Billy Cook bent the crossbar with a powerful right-foot half-volley.

Tommy Glidden was outstanding in Albion's 6-2 win over Aston Villa in March 1927. Albion's outside-right netted twice in the thrilling 6-5 special against Sunderland in March 1934

It was nip and tuck right up to the break with both sets of defenders performing gallantly, Albion's centre-half Ted Rooke doing a fine job of marking Cook.

After the interval things heated up. Carter put Albion further ahead in the fiftieth minute, ignoring appeals for offside before slipping the ball home.

Just before the hour, Davies added a third from a teasing cross from Byers and the same player made it 4-1 five minutes later after a mistake by left-half Frank Moss.

With Villa's back division now 'all at sea' Glidden cleverly stroked home a fifth goal after Jackson had spilled a ground shot from Davies, and although Villa broke away to score through Dicky York on seventy-two minutes, Short darted into space ten minutes later to grab Albion's sixth goal from another Byers cross.

This sent the Villa supporters rushing towards the exit doors and those who left early missed York's second goal, netted with five minutes remaining. Albion 'keeper Ashmore saved a 35-yard drive from Moss but couldn't gather the ball, allowing the Villa winger a simple tap in.

This was the fifty-fourth League meeting between the clubs and the victory was Albion's best up to that time. They would better it with a 7-0 win at Villa Park in 1935.

Seasiders 'Cooked' In Sun
Albion 6 Blackpool 3
League Division 2, 17 September 1927, Att. 20,203

This game was a personal triumph for centre-forward Jimmy Cookson, who scored all of Albion's six goals to set a club record which still stands today.

In bright sunshine, the Seasiders started well but fell behind in the sixth minute when Glidden crossed from the right for Cookson to fire past Fred Hobbs from 10 yards. Soon afterwards the Baggies' striker lashed another chance over the bar. To their credit, Blackpool fought back and drew level on thirty-three minutes through Sid Tufnell, who capitalised on a misunderstanding between Joe Evans and Ted Fryer to shoot past the stranded Ashmore.

Before half-time, Tufnell again went close for the visitors while at the other end, a last-ditch challenge by Arthur Tilford stopped Cookson in his tracks.

Two minutes into the second half, Blackpool's right-back Percy Thorpe handled Arthur Fitton's cross, allowing Cookson to bang in the penalty – his first for Albion.

Ten minutes later, Cookson, gliding in unnoticed, slipped home Glidden's pass to complete his first hat-trick for the club and, although Blackpool's workhorse Tufnell reduced the arrears, and then almost equalised soon afterwards, Cookson clicked into overdrive and went on a goal-spree. He scored three times in seven minutes to complete his 'second' hat-trick as Albion built up a commanding 6-1 lead.

Cookson struck from 8 yards on sixty-three minutes after Glidden and Carter had done the spadework. Two minutes later, he slotted in a rebound after his initial effort was saved and in the seventieth minute, he smashed in Wilson's pass to complete a memorable scoring afternoon.

Blackpool reduced the deficit late on through Horace Williams before Cookson thought he grabbed a seventh goal, only to be flagged offside, by a foot!

No one has equalled Cookson's record of scoring six goals in a first-class game for the Baggies – and the way defences line up now, I doubt if anyone will! Cookson set another record in 1927/28 by scoring thirty-eight League goals, beating the previous best of thirty-seven by Morris in 1919/20. W. G. Richardson eventually eclipsed Cookson's feat with thirty-nine in 1935/36.

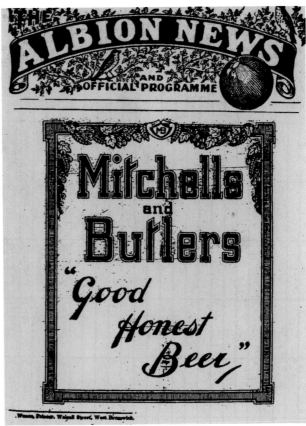

Above left: Jimmy Cookson, Albion's six-goal hero against the Seasiders.

Above right: Programme front: WBA *v.* Wolves (7-3), 28 December 1929.

Unlucky Wanderers Walloped

Albion 7 Wolverhampton Wanderers 3

League Division 2, 28 December 1929, Att. 20,211

Having beaten Wolves 4-2 at Molineux on the opening day of the season, Albion were certainly 'up for this one' as they chased their first League double over their Black Country rivals since 1910/11.

Fielding the same team that had whipped Millwall 6-1 forty-eight hours earlier, Albion started off like a house on fire, and took the lead after just three minutes when centre-half and former schoolboy international Joe Evans netted with a towering header from Glidden's right-wing corner.

Inside-left Frank Cresswell, a relatively new recruit (from Sunderland), scored a second seven minutes later with a 20-yard drive, which flew in off Wolves' full-back Harry Shaw. And although globetrotter Walter Featherby reduced the deficit in the eighteenth minute from Jimmy Deacon's pass, ninety seconds later, Stan Wood combined with W. G. Richardson (signed from Hartlepool United and playing in his first derby) to set up Glidden for Albion's third.

Unfortunately, in the thirty-fifth minute, Wolves debutant goalkeeper Billy Walker suffered a broken ankle after colliding with Glidden. Both players went for a 50-50 ball and it was the 'keeper who came off worse.

Left-half Harry Marshall took over between the posts but, after hurting his arm, he was replaced within minutes by Albert Kay who, with his first kick, sent a long clearance downfield which Bob White collected, breezed past Evans and Bill Richardson to score past Billy Light.

Albion knew they still had it all to do against plucky opponents but playing with a man short eventually took its toll on Wolves.

Carter scored Albion's fourth goal fifty seconds after the restart and in their next serious attack, on fifty-one minutes, a powerful shot from W. G. Richardson flew into the Wolves' net off the shoulder of the unlucky Shaw. At this point in the game, the referee was forced to have stern words with two Wolves defenders, Shaw and George Lax for some overzealous challenges. One on Carter by Lax certainly warranted a booking, which never came!

On the hour, Cresswell walloped in Wood's cross from the left for goal number six, and four minutes later the unmarked Carter grabbed Albion's seventh with not a Wolves player in sight!

To their credit, Wolves battled on and in the seventy-seventh minute Mark Crook broke clear to feed White for a consolation goal.

As the Wolves players tired even more, so Albion moved menacingly forward. Carter struck a 20-yarder just over, Glidden shot wide and Cresswell hit a post before time was called to end a good, solid Albion performance.

This was the fiftieth competitive game between the clubs and the 7-3 victory remains as Albion's biggest at home over their rivals.

Unique Double Completed
Albion 3 Charlton Athletic 2
League Division 2, 2 May 1931, Att. 52,415

Having beaten Midland neighbours Birmingham 2-1 in the FA Cup final the previous Saturday and Stoke 1-0 in their penultimate League game in midweek, Albion knew that another victory, this time over Charlton Athletic in their last match of the season, would see them reclaim top-flight status while at the same time they would become the first club to complete the cup and promotion double in the same season. A draw would have been good enough, but no-one knew that at the time. It was simple – go out and win!

However, the record Hawthorns League crowd was stunned when the visitors grabbed an early lead through their centre-forward Dai Astley (later to join Aston Villa) who headed home Jackie Horton's cross on eight minutes.

Shaken but not stirred, Albion gradually settled down. After efforts by Wood and W. G. Richardson had sailed over the Charlton crossbar, Glidden and twenty-year-old Teddy Sandford had both hit the woodwork and Carter's volley was saved, they deservedly drew level on thirty-seven minutes when Sandford netted with a superb lob following a right-wing corner which goalkeeper Peter Robertson failed to deal with.

But two and a half minutes later, the home crowd was silenced again as Charlton regained the lead. Horton ran in on Magee's blind side, and with a pinpoint cross, found Astley, unmarked 15 yards out whose shot flew past Harold Pearson like a bullet.

Unperturbed, Albion hit back immediately through Glidden, who clipped the ball past Robertson at the far post after W. G. Richardson had missed Wood's low cross!

In a tense atmosphere with the minutes slowly ticking by, chances came and went, with Charlton coming closest to regaining the lead when Astley raced clear only to pull his shot a yard wide. This was the turning point! After that, it was all Albion, and the all-important winning goal arrived in the sixty-eighth minute. Three Charlton defenders ventured forward to compete for a corner, but missed out. Albion's 'keeper Pearson delivered the ball long towards his entire five-man forward line, which had broken away in unison. Carter passed to Glidden on the right edge of the penalty area and, although slipping over, he got enough purchase on the ball to send it across to W. G. Richardson who, timing his run perfectly, headed the ball past Robertson amid great excitement.

There were a few tense moments during the last quarter of the game, but the Baggies comfortably closed the game down to clinch victory and so complete the unique double, a feat never achieved before or since.

At the final whistle, thousands of cheering fans raced on to the pitch to congratulate their heroes. Gathering in front of the main stand, they sang 'For they are jolly good fellows' as the players stepped into the director's box.

'It was such a great day, one I will never forget as long as I live,' said Albion's young starlet, Teddy Sandford, when I interviewed him in 1981.

Card of caricature drawings of Albion's successful double-winning 1931 squad with autographs.

Four in Five for W. G.
West Ham United 1 Albion 5
League Division 1, November 1931, Att. 20,685

Albion, skippered by Magee, could have fallen behind after forty seconds. They should have immediately taken the lead themselves, but Wood and W. G. Richardson both hesitated when free inside the penalty area.

With the action continuing, the game burst into life in spectacular fashion. Between the fifth and ninth minutes, Albion's centre-forward W. G. Richardson scored *four* times to equal the Football League record.

With spectators still entering Upton Park, Baggies' centre-half Bill Richardson, no relation, sent a long ball downfield to his namesake, whose initial shot was saved by Hammers 'keeper Ted Hufton, only for the Albion striker to smack in the rebound.

Ninety seconds later, Wood's cross from the left was driven hard and low into the net by Richardson, who then completed a quite remarkable quickfire hat-trick in the very next minute, when he burst between full-backs Reg Goodacre and Charlie Cox to smash home Glidden's pass.

With nine minutes on the clock, Richardson bagged his fourth goal from another killer pass from Wood.

This stupendous feat of scoring – four goals in five minutes, though some newspaper reports say it was four in four – equalled Jim McIntyre's record for rapid scoring for Blackburn Rovers against Everton in 1922.

With the home defence in tatters, Richardson had two more chances to score before half-time; Wood and Harry Raw saw shots saved by Hufton, while Sandford struck an upright. The nearest

W. G. Richardson, the king of Upton Park.

West Ham came to scoring was when Baggies full-back George Shaw's sliced kick flew into the safe hands of his own goalkeeper.

After the interval, West Ham did much better and were denied a penalty when Bert Trentham clearly handled, but Albion weren't finished and, on sixty-five minutes, Sandford scored a fifth goal from Raw's cross.

With the Albion duo of Jimmy Murphy and Sandford struggling with injuries, the Hammers rallied and in the seventy-second minute Jimmy Ruffell headed a consolation goal.

On this same day, Albion's 'A' team beat Dudley 10-2, while the reserves crushed Liverpool 10-1 in a Central League game at The Hawthorns, Cookson (who had lost his first team place to Richardson) scoring seven times.

Backache for Swift
Manchester City 2 Albion 7
League Division 1, 1 January 1934, Att. 27,781

Frank Swift, the giant Manchester City and future England goalkeeper, rarely conceded four goals in a game, never mind seven! But he certainly got backache in this encounter, only the third League appearance of his career.

In the preceding ten days, City had conceded thirteen goals in four games, including 8-0 and 4-1 defeats at Wolves and Derby respectively, and their defensive misery continued before a bemused Maine Road crowd, despite taking a twentieth-minute lead.

From the midway point in the first half it was virtually all Albion and, in fact, if 'Swifty' had not produced three or four fine saves, City could easily have suffered a humiliating double-figure defeat.

Albion, who had lost only one of their previous ten League matches, produced some brilliant carpet football on a near bone-hard pitch, to record their biggest away win since beating Wolves 8-0 in December 1893.

After dictating the early play, City, with a certain Matt Busby at inside-left, scored first through Alex Herd but then the tide turned dramatically. City's influential left-half Jackie Bray was carried off with a leg injury after getting his studs caught in the frozen turf, and unfortunately he stayed in the dressing room for the remainder of the first half.

In his absence, Albion immediately equalised through Welshman Walter Robbins and soon afterwards the same player found space to fire the Baggies in front.

The limping Bray returned after the break but was realistically a left-wing passenger and Albion were in no mood to hang back, going for the jugular, as they say, with all guns blazing.

W. G. Richardson became the star of the show, scoring a second-half hat-trick on twenty-three minutes to rock the Blues and give poor old 'Swifty' a day 'not' to remember!

The centre-forward whipped in a right-footer on fifty-six minutes and netted a fourth goal sixty seconds later, both following carelessness by Busby who had dropped back into Bray's position. Richardson's third came on seventy-nine minutes from Glidden's right-wing cross.

In a rare attack, the injured Bray somehow touched home a second goal for City before Carter and Sandford scored within seventy-five seconds of each other to seal an impressive away victory.

Eleven-Goal Thriller
Albion 6 Sunderland 5
League Division 1, 24 March 1934, Att. 11,889

This was a classic encounter, a great game of football, played on a heavy pitch.

Albion, attacking the Birmingham Road, struck first on fifty-five seconds when W. G. Richardson nipped round full-back Harry Shaw before bending a beauty past 'keeper Matt Middleton from an acute angle.

After Baggies centre-half Alf Ridyard had fired over, Bob Gurney equalised with a scrappy effort from Dicky Davis's low cross on seven minutes.

Back came Albion, and following Glidden's centre and a smart dummy by Richardson, Wally Boyes made it 2-1 in the fourteenth minute.

Sunderland responded, and from Jimmy Connor's pass, Raich Carter's exquisite 20-yard blast brought the scores level again midway through the half.

Then, on twenty-five minutes, Gurney edged the visitors ahead, running through a static back line to shoot low past 'keeper Ted Crowe who was deputising for Pearson.

But Albion hit back immediately through Glidden, who netted with a fierce cross-shot after Joe Carter had set him free. In Albion's next attack, Glidden repaid the compliment by delivering the perfect corner for Carter to head the Baggies in front for a third time.

Sunderland's forwards played superbly for the first twenty minutes of the second half but Albion's overworked defence stood firm and, after a period of calm, the goals flowed again. On seventy-five minutes, Sunderland's Shaw equalised with a dipping free-kick, only for Sandford to make it 5-4 with an eightieth-minute penalty after Bill Murray had fouled Boyes.

Glidden's floating cross eluded everybody and bounced in off the post to give Albion a two goal lead with five minutes to play – leaving just enough time for Gurney to complete his hat-trick and so end a quite brilliant match.

It was a pity that under 12,000 spectators saw it – the second lowest of the season at The Hawthorns.

Seven Up the Villa!
Aston Villa 0 Albion 7
League Division 1, 19 October 1935, Att. 43,411

For Albion supporters, victory at Villa Park is always sweet, but in 1935 it was much more than that, as they outplayed the foe from Aston with a magnificent display of attacking football.

Villa had been struggling all season, conceding twenty-three goals in ten League games, including seven at Middlesbrough. Nevertheless, they still had some good players, but there was no stopping Albion who produced an exhilarating display to tear the home defence apart.

The Baggies fans were celebrating as early as the seventh minute when W. G. Richardson smashed in Jack Mahon's right-wing cross. And fifty seconds later, it was 2-0 when Wood fired home after good work by Richardson.

With a strong wind behind them, Albion drove forward in numbers. On twenty-five minutes Richardson netted a beauty from another Mahon cross and four minutes before the interval, Mahon turned in Wood's delightful pass for number four. It was much of the same after the break, with Albion attacking and Villa defending, desperately at times.

Right: Jack Sankey, who played his part in the great win at Villa Park, 1935.

Far right: W. G. Richardson bagged four goals again, in Albion's crushing 7-0 win at Villa Park in October 1935.

In the seventy-fifth minute, Jack Sankey increased Albion's lead, picking up the pieces after Villa's 'keeper Fred Biddlestone had fumbled Richardson's low shot.

The influential Carter made Albion's sixth goal for Richardson on seventy-seven minutes and the centre-forward gleefully netted his fourth of the game just sixty seconds later, scuffing Wood's cross in from 6 yards.

In fact, Richardson should have equalled Cookson's scoring record for most goals in a game, but fluffed two easy chances as Villa gave up.

This was Albion's best away win in League football since hammering Wolves 8-0 in 1893 and remains as their best on the road to this day.

Rovers Rumbled

Albion 8 Blackburn Rovers 1

League Division 1, 18 January 1936, Att. 16,464

After scoring ten goals in their previous two home games, Albion kept up the momentum against bottom-of-the-table Blackburn, whose defence during the first half of the season, had taken a right old battering!

Albion started superbly, netting five times in the first twenty minutes as the visitors were given a lesson in how to play forceful but controlled football.

On seven minutes, Rovers' defenders Jimmy Gorman and Arnold Whiteside kicked wildly at the ball together. It flew to W. G. Richardson who netted comfortably.

Fifty seconds later, Mahon whipped in number two after some clever play by right-half Sankey and Sandford.

Richardson created Albion's third goal for Walter Robbins in the tenth minute and five minutes later Mahon, cutting inside, scored a fourth in off the post.

In the twentieth minute, a stinging drive from Sandford was spilled by 'keeper Cliff Binns, allowing Sankey a simple tap in for number five before Jack Thompson netted a dubious penalty for Rovers on thirty minutes.

Albion continued to dominate after the break and in two quickfire attacks hotshot Richardson scored twice more, his twenty-fourth and twenty-fifth League goals of the season, to complete his hat-trick and give Albion a commanding and unbeatable 7-1 lead with still half an hour left to play. Despite several near misses, the crowd had to wait until the very last minute before Albion scored their eighth goal. Wood's cross was flicked on by Robbins to Mahon, who fired home his third goal with aplomb.

This was the first time two Albion players had scored hat-tricks in the same League game since 1893. Sad Rovers were relegated after conceding ninety-six goals.

Sweet Revenge
Albion 6 Liverpool 1
League Division 1, 1 February 1936, Att. 23,080

Earlier in the season Liverpool had thrashed Albion 5-0 at Anfield, but this time it was the visitors who had red faces!

Having scored a hat-trick seven days earlier, the lively W. G. Richardson fired Albion in front on four minutes, only for Jack Balmer to equalise six minutes later after a weak header by Baggies full-back Trentham.

After that, however, it was all Albion, and with the visitors' defence taking a real pasting, the unchallenged Mahon made 2-1 on fifteen minutes.

Richardson (twice), Carter (back in action following injury), Sandford and left-half Jack Rix all came close to increasing the lead as Liverpool struggled to get out of their own half.

After the interval, Albion revved up their engine again, and after missing the target from 6 yards, Richardson completed his second hat-trick in successive games with unstoppable efforts in the fifty-second and fifty-ninth minutes.

With Liverpool hardly threatening, the excellent Wood netted twice more in the last seven minutes to send the Merseysiders packing.

Far left: Teddy Sandford defended stubbornly against Liverpool in 1936.

Left: Wally Boyes had a fine game in Albion's 6-4 win over Sunderland in February 1937, scoring one of the goals.

Wearsiders Concede Six Again
Albion 6 Sunderland 4
League Division 1, 27 February 1937 , Att. 25,267

Three years earlier, Albion beat Sunderland 6-5 in an eleven-goal thriller; this game was just as exciting, with the Baggies narrow winners once again.

After a negative first half-hour on a heavy pitch, the goals started to flow as W. G. Richardson put Albion in front. The champions responded and in double-quick time Eddie Burbanks equalised and Raich Carter drove the visitors ahead.

Albion went straight downfield, Harry 'Popeye' Jones was fouled, but Sandford's well-struck penalty was saved by Johnny Mapson.

A minute after the break, Wally Boyes made it 2-2 before Lol Coen, making only his third senior appearance, put the Baggies in front from Jones' flick. After Carter had levelled again for the visitors, Albion won a second penalty when Coen was fouled. This time full-back Cecil Shaw almost tore a hole in the net with his powerful spot-kick.

Albion extended their lead to 5-3 on seventy-two minutes when Jones netted with a 12-yard toe-poke, and eight minutes later the same player bagged number six. Sunderland rallied and winger Len Duns, who would assist the Baggies during the Second World War, made it 6-4 before Carter saw his late penalty saved by Baggies 'keeper Jimmy Adams.

Albion and Sunderland played each other twelve times at League level between 1932 and 1938 and in those games a total of sixty goals were scored.

Ike Spikes County
Newport County 2 Albion 7
League Division 2, 28 September 1946, Att. 17,614

Tipton-born centre-forward Ike Clarke became Albion's first post-Second World War hat-trick hero with a four-timer in this splendid win in stifling heat at Somerton Park.

Ex-Albion full-back Jim Southam deflected George Tranter's well-struck shot past his own 'keeper Bill Brookin to give the visitors a fourth-minute lead, and soon afterwards Ray Barlow, making his Baggies' League debut, had a goal disallowed for offside.

Albion's lead was cancelled out on fifteen minutes by Reg Mogford, who netted after good work by Miller Craddock, but two attacks and two minutes later, Barlow put Albion 2-1 ahead. Then, straight from the restart, County's inside-right Ken Wookey forced Albion's goalkeeper Jim Sanders into a fine one-handed save.

Albion had several chances to add to their tally, but had to wait until the fiftieth minute before scoring again, Stan Butler dribbling his way through a lazy defence to set up Billy Elliott who simply couldn't miss!

Clarke netted the first of his four goals from 10 yards halfway through the second half and after Barlow and Elliott had seen efforts saved by Brookin, Ted Davis pulled one back for the home side, only for Clarke to head in Elliott's cross to restore Albion's three-goal advantage.

It was all Albion at this juncture and their superiority showed as four chances were created in quick succession, only for Jimmy Duggan, Elliott (twice) and Barlow to miss them all.

Above left: A caricature drawing of 'Ike' Clarke, who scored 4 goals in Albion's 7-2 win at Newport on 28 September 1946.

Above right: Programme front: Newport County *v.* WBA (2-7), 1946/47.

But the irresistible Clarke wasn't so lenient and when the ball dropped to him on seventy-six minutes, the bustling striker rapped in his hat-trick goal, following up soon afterwards with a fourth as County defenders tired.

Albion had to wait until September 1953 (at Newcastle) before they would again score seven goals in an away League game.

Walsh Carves Up the Avenue
Albion 7 Bradford Park Avenue 1
League Division 2, 16 April 1949, 39,241

Promotion-chasing Albion thrilled a sun-baked Hawthorns crowd with some superb attacking football and they were certainly not flattered by this big win.

Irish international Dave Walsh was the game's outstanding player, scoring four goals for the Baggies as time and again the Bradford defence was cut to ribbons.

After Jack Haines had twice gone close for Albion, Walsh opened the scoring on fifteen minutes, firing in Barlow's brilliant forward pass.

Six minutes later Walsh added a second, drilling home a penalty kick after Bradford left-half Will Elliott had handled.

Albion, driving forward in numbers with Barlow at the helm, went 3-0 up on twenty-five minutes when Haines drove in a 25-yarder high into the net after a short pass from left-winger Hugh Morrow, and just before the half-hour mark Walsh completed his hat-trick. Taking Paddy Ryan's pass in his stride, he raced clear of the defence, rounded goalkeeper Chick Farr and slotted the ball into the net with ease.

There was more to come before the break when Haines, in acres of space, put away winger Elliott's cross to make it five.

Albion ended the half with ten men, Elliott having gone off with a damaged ankle, but he was back at the start of the second period and immediately set up a sixth goal for Morrow.

It was now one-way traffic and Walsh should have scored again before Bradford, in a rare attack, clawed a goal back through George Ainsley, who rose between Joe Kennedy and Jack Vernon to head in Gerald Henry's cross on fifty-one minutes.

Albion's goalkeeper Sanders then earned his corn with good saves from Ainsley and Bill Deplidge.

At this point Bradford – with several of their players looking leg weary – chose to sit back, damage limitation really, and Albion were awarded a string of free-kicks, two of which resulted in Walsh and Haines striking the woodwork. Although it was virtually all Albion, they had to wait until the eighty-fourth minute before scoring their seventh goal, Walsh turning in Elliott's low centre with consummate ease.

This four-timer took Walsh's goal tally for the season to twenty-six (twenty-one in the League) as Albion moved to within striking distance of the Second Division leaders Southampton.

This was also the last time Albion played Park Avenue and the emphatic win was their biggest over the Yorkshire club in twenty-six League matches.

Promotion Victory
Leicester City 0 Albion 3
League Division 2, 5 May 1949, Att. 35,800

With two away games left to play at the end of the season, Albion knew that victory in one of them would earn them promotion back to the First Division.

The trip to relegation candidates and beaten FA Cup finalists Leicester was first up and a huge crowd assembled at Filbert Street to see it. In fact, the gates were closed long before kick-off with almost 36,000 packed inside, including a large contingent of Baggies supporters.

Straight from the kick-off Albion looked dangerous, but it was City who had the first chance, Mal Griffiths lifting Jack Lee's cross onto the Albion bar. The ball came down near the line and was hacked clear by Jack Vernon.

In the twelfth minute, the visitors took the lead. Kennedy, playing at inside-right, rose highest to head down Paddy Ryan's free-kick for Walsh to score in off a post from close range.

Fourteen minutes later it was 2-0 when Kennedy, unmarked, glided home Arthur Smith's left-wing corner.

The 1948/49 promotion-winning squad.

Holding on to their lead comfortably, Albion dictated the play for long periods but had to wait until the sixty-fourth minute before adding to their goal tally. And it was the tireless Barlow who scored it, finishing off a three-man move with an angled drive just inside the post.

Thereafter, Walsh (twice) and Smith missed chances to increase Albion's commanding lead with City looking totally disinterested.

When the final whistle sounded, hundreds of delighted Baggies' supporters charged onto the pitch to carry their heroes shoulder-high from the scene of their triumph. Albion had been out of the top flight since 1927. 'Welcome back' was the banner headline of the following day's local newspaper.

Champions Walloped

Albion 5 Portsmouth 0
League Division 1, 9 September 1950, Att. 34,460

Albion completely annihilated the League champions in this one-sided encounter at The Hawthorns.

However, despite bossing practically the whole of the first half, the deadlock wasn't broken until the forty-second minute when centre-forward Walsh netted with a superbly executed overhead kick from Elliott's right-wing cross.

Forty-five seconds later Elliott banged in a second from an intelligent pass by Cyril Williams, and three minutes after the interval, Williams headed home Ronnie Allen's perfect cross from the left.

To their credit, the visitors kept plugging away and both wingers, Peter Harris and Jack Froggatt, had chances, but it was evident that they were missing the strength through the middle of former Albion marksman Ike Clarke.

With their defence looking solid, especially Jack Vernon, Albion pressed forward and only two fine saves by Pompey's reserve 'keeper Ron Humpston prevented Walsh and Allen from finding the net.

Eventually, the impressive Smith stroked home a fourth goal from the inside-left position and the same player rounded things off with another brilliant strike in the eighty-seventh minute as Pompey caved in.

Thirteen months later, Albion again beat Portsmouth 5-0, making it nine home wins out of ten since the first meeting in 1931. In those ten games, Albion scored thirty-two goals.

Easter Double

Wolverhampton Wanderers 1 Albion 4
League Division 1, 15 April 1952, Att. 35,940

Having won 2-1 at The Hawthorns twenty-four hours earlier, thanks to Johnny Nicholls' late goal, Albion completed the double over their Black Country rivals with this superb 4-1 victory, their first at Molineux for twenty years.

To be fair, Albion dominated this Easter Tuesday afternoon contest from start to finish and should have won by a much bigger margin, although some credit must go to England goalkeeper Bert Williams, who pulled off at least four terrific saves.

Allen, a scoring debutant against Wolves two years earlier, netted Albion's opener with a sharp right-footed drive on twenty-one minutes, and after a lot of goalmouth activity at the Wolves end of the pitch, Nicholls put Albion 2-0 up with a scorching cross-shot from 20 yards on thirty-eight minutes.

However, with half-time approaching, it came as a bit of a shock when South African defender Eddie Stuart, making his debut as an emergency centre-forward, headed Wolves back into the game.

On the hour, after Albion had moved up a gear, Allen made it 3-1 with a thumping left-footed free-kick, which zoomed past Williams like a rocket from fully 20 yards. Then, after Nicholls had fired into the side-netting, Allen completed his hat-trick from close quarters and, in doing so, surpassed Walsh's post-war record of twenty-eight League goals in a season.

Allen ended 1951/52 with thirty-five League and cup goals in his locker – the most by an Albion player since W. G. Richardson's tally of forty in 1935/36.

Boxing Day Special

Sheffield Wednesday 4 Albion 5
League Division 1, 26 December 1952, Att. 59,398

This was an amazing match, end to end action throughout and nine goals to boot. In front of a bumper Hillsborough crowd, it was Wednesday who struck first, Dennis Woodhead scoring on five minutes after chasing Cyril Turton's long pass through the middle.

Albion responded, and five minutes later the outstanding Barlow moved menacingly forward, collected Ryan's shot pass and fired hard and low past Ron Capewell from 30 yards.

Wednesday counter-attacked, and within fifty seconds their England international inside-left Redfern Froggatt put them back in front with a spectacular diving header from Jackie Marriott's cross.

Far left: Ronnie Allen scored goals galore for Albion including a hat-trick at Wolves in April 1952, and a four-timer *v.* Cardiff City in November 1953 ... plus many more trebles during his eleven years at the Hawthorns.

Left: Johnny Nicholls helped Albion to a thrilling win at Hillsborough, 26 December 1952.

It was great stuff and it continued as Albion drew level for a second time in the fourteenth minute when Wednesday's left-back Norman Curtis diverted Allen's shot past his own 'keeper.

Close to half-time Woodhead, pulling clear of Stan Rickaby and Jimmy Dudley, eased Wednesday into a 3-2 lead. And it got worse for Albion when, two minutes after the break, Derek Dooley added a fourth for the hooting Owls when he darted between Kennedy and Dudley to get on the end of Jackie Sewell's square pass.

Albion roared back and were gifted a second own-goal on fifty-three minutes. With Allen and Nicholls ready to pounce, Wednesday's right-half Eddie Gannon misjudged Ryan's clever centre and headed the ball past Capewell from near the penalty spot.

The last half an hour was full of goalmouth incidents. Wednesday came close to extending their lead through Woodhead and Dooley, while Allen, Nicholls and Frank Griffin could have scored for Albion.

With ten minutes remaining, Nicholls popped up inside the area to equalise and soon afterwards Allen's well-struck effort took a slight deflection off Owls right-back Vince Kenny and Albion had won.

This was a tremendous victory for the Baggies who, amazingly, just twenty-four hours later, were defeated 1-0 by Wednesday at The Hawthorns, Dooley scoring the all-important goal. Such is football – anything can happen when least expected!

Barlow Shines on Tyneside
Newcastle United 3 Albion 5
League Division 1, 1 January 1953, Att. 48,944

Albion made it ten goals in two away games with this excellent victory at St James' Park, which was inspired by the elegant Barlow who ran the show from midfield.

After soaking up early pressure, Albion took the lead on ten minutes when Ryan scored with a crisp left-footer from Barlow's square pass.

England star and home favourite Jackie Milburn equalised in the twenty-sixth minute, only for George Lee to lob in Albion's second goal three minutes later when United's 'keeper Ronnie Simpson lost his bearings.

However, on thirty-five minutes, left-winger Bobby Mitchell, cutting inside Rickaby, squared things up again at 2-2 with a thumping shot which flew low past Norman Heath's right hand.

Before the interval, Milburn and Allen both had shots saved by the respective 'keepers and following a series of corner-kicks at opposite ends of the field, Nicholls scored from 2 yards to give Albion a 3-2 lead just past the hour mark. Then, in Albion's next attack, the same player fired over.

This miss could have proved costly for Albion when Welshman Reg Davies levelled things up for Newcastle on seventy-one minutes. But Griffin had other ideas. The winger anticipated Ryan's forward pass and, before left-back Alf McMichael could react, he had banged the ball home to edge Albion 4-3 ahead on seventy-seven minutes.

Pushing men forward, inevitably Newcastle left holes at the back, and with nine minutes remaining Barlow scored Albion's fifth and match-clinching goal.

This victory took the Baggies to the top of the First Division table; they eventually finished in fourth place with Newcastle sixteenth.

Scintillating Baggies
Newcastle United 3 Albion 7
League Division 1, 16 September 1953, Att. 58,075

Albion reached the crowning glory of football perfection with a magnificent display of attacking football, which completely destroyed what one thought was a well-equipped Newcastle team. At the end of the game, the appreciative home supporters stood to a man and cheered Vic Buckingham's players off the field.

Allen, making his 150th senior appearance for the Baggies, and in sight of his seventy-fifth first-class goal for the club, had a header disallowed, struck a post and wasn't at all happy to have

George Lee scored in four successive League games against Newcastle.

a clear penalty shout turned down, before finally netting with a 30-yard drive on thirty-three minutes after some intricate play involving Barlow and Dudley and a final touch from Ryan.

Two minutes later Nicholls, reacting brilliantly, scored from close range after Allen's header had been pushed onto the bar by goalkeeper Simpson. Shortly before half-time Allen, with a quick turn and shot, scored again with the help of an angled deflection off centre-half Frank Brennan, Simpson diving the wrong way.

Early in the second half, Vic Keeble pulled a goal back for Newcastle (from George Hannah's pass) and as Albion retreated, left-winger Mitchell cut the deficit to one on the hour.

But back came Albion, and after a swift, purposeful move involving Barlow and Allen, master poacher Nicholls stole in behind right-back George Cowell to make it 4-2 in the sixty-fifth minute.

United rallied again, and the dangerous Mitchell made it 4-3 with just over a quarter of an hour remaining. But Albion, strong and resilient, went into overdrive and scored three more quality goals in the space of nine minutes to clinch a brilliant win.

On seventy-six minutes, Nicholls completed his first Albion hat-trick after charging through the middle to collect Barlow's defence-splitting pass; Ryan lashed in number six soon afterwards, and with five minutes remaining Frank Griffin out-paced Ron Batty to score Albion's seventh to round off an absolutely stupendous performance – their best on the road in the top flight since hammering Aston Villa 7-0 in 1935.

This took Albion's goal tally in three successive visits at St James' Park to sixteen, while the last time Newcastle conceded seven at home was against Portsmouth in 1939.

Allen Grabs the Glory
Albion 6 Cardiff City 1
League Division 1, 21 November 1953, Att. 39,618

Hotshot centre-forward Allen, who had sat on the bench as an England reserve watching the infamous 6-3 defeat by Hungary a few days earlier, showed the selectors what he could do with a brilliant four-timer against the Bluebirds.

This, in fact, was his third hat-trick in four home games. He was on fire.

However, Albion, without injured right-back Rickaby, whose absence brought to an end a run of 143 consecutive League appearances, found themselves a goal down after just six minutes when Jack Chisholm, unmarked at the far post, headed home Dougie Blair's deep cross from the left.

Nicholls should have equalised immediately, but was happy to see his partner Allen level things up from close range on fourteen minutes. Lee's shot cannoned off Blair and dropped into his path and, thinking he was offside, Allen simply rolled the ball slowly over the line, only to turn round and spot the referee pointing to the centre circle.

After Baggies 'keeper Norman Heath had produced a superb save from Wilf Grant, Allen cleverly made it 2-1 from Ryan's pass on twenty-eight minutes and the centre-forward struck for a third time seven minutes later from another Ryan assist to complete his hat-trick.

The former Port Vale striker's fourth goal arrived six minutes after the break, and once again Ryan was involved. The Irishman slipped the ball between Stan Montgomery and Colin Baker for Allen to collect and fire low into the net with what can lonely be described as a 'daisy-cutter', Howells being completely wrong-footed.

Thereafter Nicholls, Lee and Griffin all missed chances and Cardiff's right-back Alan Harrington knocked a back-pass against his own post before Nicholls got in the act with Albion's fifth goal on

Above left: Ronnie Allen, who scored four against Cardiff City, 21 November 1953.

Above right: Stan Rickaby, who scored with a rocket in the Sheffield Wednesday game.

seventy-nine minutes, following up four minutes later with number six from Griffin's cross from the right. Just before the final whistle, Allen struck the outside of Howells' left-hand upright.

This was Albion's biggest home League win for four years.

Great Comeback
Albion 4 Sheffield Wednesday 2
League Division 1, 13 February 1954, Att. 38,475

Albion, despite being without Barlow, who had been quite outstanding, went three points clear of Wolves at the top of the table with this hard-earned win.

After Lee contrived to miss an open goal in Albion's first attack, a poor defensive header allowed Jackie Sewell to slip in winger Dennis Woodhead to score for the Owls after just two minutes.

It got worse for the stunned home supporters when, ninety seconds later, Jack Shaw fired in Alan Finney's low cross, which had somehow found its way across a crowded penalty area. Albion were at sixes and sevens, but they regrouped and peppered the Wednesday goal for a good ten minutes, Nicholls (twice), Allen, Griffin and Dudley, who bent the crossbar with a thunderous drive, all going agonisingly close.

Finally, after continuous pressure, Nicholls reduced the arrears on twenty-seven minutes and, five minutes later, another one of Dudley's long range efforts flew in off centre-half Barry Butler and past 'keeper Brian Ryalls and Vince Kenny for the equaliser.

The tide had turned. Albion were in charge, and on forty-nine minutes full-back Rickaby, charging down the right flank in support of Griffin, hammered the ball home from 35 yards to put Albion in front.

Four minutes later, Ryan, who was working his socks (and boots) off, banged home Lee's cross – 4-2, game over, although there was ample time for Allen to shoot over (by a mile) and Ryan to head wide.

Albion's manager Buckingham said after the game, 'It was a great recovery but an under par performance. This happens occasionally.'

Johnny on the Spot

Albion 6 Leicester City 4
League Division 1, 25 September 1954, Att. 48,422

Five goals were scored in each half of this end-to-end Hawthorns thriller.

Allen maintained his goal-a-game record by giving Albion a twelfth-minute lead with a 25-yarder that flew into the net off Stan Milburn.

Nine minutes later it was 2-0 when Griffin's wobbling high-cross deceived 'keeper Adam Dickson and dropped in just under the bar. On the half hour, Nicholls powered in a third from a superb centre by the menacing Griffin.

Leicester hit back with a goal from Derek Hines on thirty-four minutes (from Dave Richardson's pass) but five minutes before the interval, on-the-spot Nicholls flashed in Albion's fourth from the edge of the box.

After shots from Allen and Lee had crashed off the Leicester crossbar and Nicholls had put both rebounds over the top, ex-Baggies star Arthur Rowley reduced the arrears to 4-2 on the hour and Mal Griffiths brought the scores even closer with a third for Leicester three minutes later.

Far left: Johnny Nicholls scored hat-tricks in Albion's 7-3 win at Newcastle in September 1953 and in the 6-4 win over Leicester City a year later.

Left: Frank Griffin scored his only hat-trick for Albion against Manchester City in 1957.

Thankfully Albion found another gear and Lee swept in a fifth on seventy-five minutes before Nicholls completed his second hat-trick for the club on eighty-one minutes.

Battling to the death, Leicester claimed a fourth goal with five minutes remaining, when Johnny Morris swept in a Griffiths cross.

Albion lost the return fixture 6-3 at Filbert Street, meaning that nineteen goals were scored in two matches between the clubs in 1954/55. Beat that for value!

'M' For Massacre
Albion 9 Manchester City 2
League Division 1, 21 September 1957, Att. 26,222

With top-scorer Allen missing, Albion still went goal crazy, completely destroying Manchester City's much vaunted 'M' plan.

Don Howe fired the Baggies ahead on twenty-one minutes, his 35-yard drive deflecting off Keith Marsden.

Fifteen minutes later it was 2-0 when Brian Whitehouse's outstretched leg diverted Barlow's low shot past City's static 'keeper John Savage.

City pulled a goal back in the thirty-ninth minute through Roy Clarke but two minutes later, Griffin, collecting Barlow's astute lob, made it 3-1.

Ten minutes into the second half, Fionan Fagan dragged City back to 3-2, but fifty seconds later Savage could only parry Griffin's shot into the air, allowing Bobby Robson to head home (4-2).

After Ken Barnes (father of future Baggies star Peter) had missed a fifty-eighth-minute penalty, Griffin dribbled past four defenders to score a brilliant fifth goal for Albion on sixty-one minutes.

Roy Horobin then netted a beauty to make it 6-2 with twenty minutes remaining and after he was fouled by Dave Ewing on seventy-nine minutes, Howe made it 7-2 from the spot. Four minutes from time, Griffin completed his hat-trick from Horobin's pass and with the referee poised to call time, Ewing conceded a second penalty by flooring Derek Kevan who promptly got up to blast the ball past Savage.

This remains as Albion's biggest-ever League win at The Hawthorns.

Babes Beaten
Albion 4 Manchester United 3
League Division 1, 26 October 1957, Att. 52,839

This was a tremendously exciting match, packed with quality football.

The opening four goals were all headers. The first and third were scored by United and England centre-forward Tommy Taylor in the seventh and thirteenth minutes, each one after Albion's defence had failed to prevent wingers Johnny Berry and David Pegg from delivering well-driven crosses from the flanks.

The second and fourth goals came from Albion's inside-right Robson, in the sixteenth and twenty-seventh minutes. Once again, there was indifferent marking inside the danger zone by static United's defenders, simply because Robson very rarely scored with his head!

After some thrilling goalmouth activity at both ends of the pitch, a fine Kevan strike gave the Baggies a 3-2 half-time lead they just about deserved.

Above left: Bobby Robson netted with two great headers against Manchester United, 26 October 1957.

Above right: Programme for Blues *v.* Albion, 1957 (5-3 win).

The action continued in the second half, and after Albion's 'keeper Sanders had dived to his left to save Berry's penalty, awarded when future United player Maurice Setters had handled Billy Whelan's shot on the line (missed by the referee but spotted by a linesman), Allen swooped to make it 4-2 in the sixth-sixth minute, only for Whelan to reduce the deficit thirteen minutes from time.

Late on, with the visitors pressing strongly for an equaliser, Barlow should have made it 5-3, and then with his last kick of the game, Taylor came mighty close to saving a point for the Busby Babes.

This was an impressive win for Albion over the League champions and later in the season they would score another four goals against United.

Great, Late Christmas Present

Birmingham City 3 Albion 5
League Division 1, 26 December 1957, Att. 48,396

After getting off to a slow start, this local derby burst into life and produced capital entertainment for a bumper crowd at St Andrew's.

Neither side had threatened, not even put in a shot, before Albion went ahead in the twenty-fifth minute. From the last of three successive corners, Kevan flicked on Griffin's flag-kick to Robson, whose shot was diverted past goalkeeper Gil Merrick by Blues full-back Brian Farmer.

The home side, fresh from victory over rivals Aston Villa, hit back strongly and after a couple of close shaves, Eddie Brown equalised from Noel Kinsey's pass just before half-time.

Four minutes after the resumption, Robson collected Barlow's pass and scythed through the Blues' defence to score a beauty (2-1) and with Albion now on top, Kevan headed a third goal in off the crossbar from Griffin's free-kick on sixty-six minutes.

After Dick Neal had luckily reduced the deficit from a corner on seventy-one minutes, Kennedy and Griffin set up Kevan for Albion's fourth seven minutes later.

Although Harry Hooper banged in a penalty for Blues on eighty-three minutes, awarded for deliberate handball by Setters, Allen scored Albion's match-clinching fifth goal soon afterwards with a wonderful overhead kick.

Cyril Chapman, reporting in the *Birmingham Post & Mail*, said, 'This was an impressive win by Albion who will still offer a stern challenge to Wolverhampton Wanderers.' As it happened, Wolves won the League title, while Albion came fourth!

A Real Bobby Dazzler
Albion 5 Burnley 1
League Division 1, 28 December 1957, Att. 38,386

With this solid victory at The Hawthorns, Albion made it ten goals in two games – and seven days later it would become fifteen in three after Manchester City had been crushed 5-1 in an FA Cup tie.

Having netted twice at Birmingham on Boxing Day, Robson doubled that tally with a four-timer against the Clarets who, despite taking an eighteenth-minute lead through Brian Pilkington, were never at the races as Albion dominated proceedings, especially after the interval. Visiting goalkeeper Colin McDonald had pulled off five superb first-half saves, but was left helpless when Robson equalised with a cracking shot from Don Howe's cross on fifty-four minutes.

Although in control, Albion had to wait until the sixty-fifth minute before moving ahead, Robson scoring after Setters had flicked on Allen's corner.

Two minutes later Kevan, 30 yards out, thundered the ball home to give Albion a 3-1 lead; Robson completed his hat-trick ten minutes from time after Allen had touched on a Setters pass; and in the eighty-fourth minute the England international, capped for the first time against France a month earlier, drove home his fourth goal and Albion's fifth from Lee's free-kick.

Surprisingly, ace marksmen Astle, Regis and Taylor never scored four goals in a game for Albion, but Robson did. Well, he was a fine player.

Post Munich Nightmare For United
Manchester United 0 Albion 4
League Division 1, March 1958, Att. 63,479

This game was played a month after the Munich air disaster and three days after Albion had lost 1-0 to United in an FA Cup quarter-final replay at Old Trafford.

Bobby Robson was bang in form
with four goals in the 5-1 win over
Burnley in 1957.

Albion, unlucky to lose that replay, played brilliantly on the same pitch and tore the Reds apart time and again.

After Kevan had gone close early on, Allen opened the scoring on eight minutes with one of his typical quality strikes from just outside the penalty area. The centre-forward then fired over, while Kevan, Robson and left-winger Horobin all had chances to increase Albion's lead as United came under severe pressure.

In fact, all the lacklustre Reds could offer was a weak header from centre-forward Alex Dawson and a half-hit shot by Colin Webster.

Ten minutes before half-time Albion went 2-0 up when Allen's sharp, crisp effort was turned past his own 'keeper (Harry Gregg) by full-back Ian Greaves.

After being denied a clear penalty, Barlow shot straight at Gregg as Albion continued to press forward and the unstoppable Kevan made it 3-0 in the fifty-seventh minute.

Robson and Brian Whitehouse, the latter playing on the right wing in place of Griffin, who sadly broke his leg in the fifth-round FA Cup replay with Sheffield United, should have found the net again before Allen wrapped things up with a spot-kick ten minutes from time.

This, without doubt, was a magnificent win for Albion, their second at Old Trafford in five visits but only their third in thirteen. They would return however, and win their next two League games on United soil, by 2-1 in October 1958 and 3-2 in December 1960.

City Get the Blues!
Birmingham City 0 Albion 6
League Division 1, 3 September 1958, Att. 35,983

Inadequate and dazed, Blues were outplayed and in the end were literally 'washed' away at rain-soaked St Andrew's by a very impressive Albion side that got off to a great start! In their third attack, former Leicester City winger Derek Hogg crossed from the left for Allen to volley home on seven minutes.

DAVID
BURNSIDE
INSIDE-FORWARD

DAVID
BURNSIDE

BALL JUGGLER
DAVID HAS PLAYED
OVER 100 LEAGUE
GAMES FOR ALBION

Bazooka ★
THE CHEW OF CHAMPIONS

Davey Burnside mesmerised Blues.

Albion's lively attack kept the unhappy Blues defenders on their toes and it came as no surprise when Davey Burnside cracked in a second goal past the unsighted Merrick from the edge of the penalty area on thirty-three minutes.

Two minutes later, Kevan side-stepped three defenders to fire in number three and straight from the kick-off Jimmy Campbell scrambled in a fourth goal after a melee inside the 6-yard box.

It was all Albion who confirmed their superiority, with a fifth goal two minutes into the second half. Campbell raced past three opponents, sitting Ken Green and Graham Sissons on their backsides, before cutting inside Neal and letting rip with a real beauty which flew low past former England 'keeper Merrick.

With the Blues looking totally bedraggled, some smart adjustment by Burnside enabled him to secure a sixth goal on sixty-seven minutes after Kevan's shot had been blocked on the line. And before the final whistle, the overworked Merrick had to pull off three fine saves, two quite superb from Kevan and Allen, as Albion bombarded the home goal. This made in eleven goals for Albion in two visits to St Andrew's – and there was more, much more, to come!

Everton Flattened by the Tank
Albion 6 Everton 2
League Division 1, 19 March 1960, Att. 24,887

This was, without doubt, Derek Kevan's match, as the burly striker came mighty close to equalling – even breaking – Jimmy Cookson's club record of six goals in a game, set thirty-three years earlier, in 1927. He did, however, emulate Fred Morris's 1919 achievement of scoring five times in a League match.

Trailing 2-0 to Bobby Collins and Roy Vernon goals inside the first thirteen minutes, Albion slowly but surely gained control and eventually won the game in style with Kevan banging in a five-timer, including four in the last twenty minutes.

After a close range tap-in by Collins and a precise lob from Vernon Albion, who had looked like amateurs as Everton dominated early on, had to do something quickly, and having seen Allen miss two great chances to reduce the arrears, Kevan, from Burnside's clever pass, finally struck on the half an hour.

Everton, though, were proving tough opponents, and twice Albion's Scottish goalkeeper Jock Wallace prevented Mickey Lill and Jimmy Harris from adding further goals.

With less than twenty minutes remaining and the home fans getting restless, Albion equalised when Kevan, chesting down Burnside's chipped pass, fired his shot low and hard past Albert Dunlop.

Two minutes later, 'The Tank' bagged his second hat-trick of the season to edge Albion 3-2 in front. Allen's shot flew into the air off a defender, for Kevan to rush in and head the ball into the net from a yard.

Ten minutes from time, Burnside got on the score-sheet with Albion's fourth goal with a fine shot from 20 yards, before the star of the show Kevan smacked home goal number five with a terrific left-footed piledriver from Burnside's assist on eighty-two minutes.

Five minutes later, Baggies hero Kevan brought up the half-dozen with a clever hook shot after the impressive Burnside had slipped the ball to him in front of goal, and soon afterwards saw another goal-bound effort saved by Dunlop.

This was a wonderful personal achievement for Kevan who went on to score a total of twenty-nine goals this season, including his 100th for the club.

The Allen & Kevan Show
Birmingham City 1 Albion 7
League Division 1, 18 April 1960, Att. 28,685

Albion made it a total of eighteen goals scored against Blues in three consecutive League visits to St Andrew's, and in truth, the final score of this one-sided encounter could have been 10-1, even 12-1, so well did the Baggies play.

Surprisingly Blues scored first, Johnny Gordon steering in Gordon Astall's fourth-minute corner. But the home defence had been leaking goals all season, and six minutes later Kevan nodded Derek Hogg's cross down for Allen to slam in the equaliser.

Five minutes before the interval, Albion were ahead, Allen firing the ball high into the net after his initial shot had been saved by Johnny Schofield.

Two minutes later, Albion's centre-half Kennedy carried the ball 50 yards upfield, before setting up Alec Jackson who, taking one touch, scored from 20 yards. This was a terrific goal.

Kevan netted Albion's fourth on fifty-seven minutes with a powerful shot following a strong, determined run, and six minutes later the burly striker netted again, this time with a bullet header from Hogg's free-kick.

Albion continued to pour forward, and ninety seconds from time Kevan completed his hat-trick after robbing George Allen.

In the ninety-first minute, the Blues full-back then tripped Robson, allowing his namesake, Ronnie, to complete his hat-trick from the penalty spot. If luck had been on Kevan's side, one feels he would have scored at least another couple of goals.

Not since 1936, when Mahon and W. G. Richardson hit trebles against Blackburn, had two Albion players scored hat-tricks in the same League game. While Allen and Kevan were hat-trick heroes at St Andrew's, coincidentally, 5 miles away at The Hawthorns, Andy Aitken and Jack Lovatt notched hat-tricks for Albion's second XI.

Twenty-four hours later, for the third successive season, Blues plundered a point at The Hawthorns. Football's a funny old game…

Allen's Last Treble

Albion 6 Manchester City 3
League Division 1, 24 September 1960, Att. 25,163

Albion and City produced a feast of football and it was hard on the visitors to lose such a wonderful match, which had everything. Indeed, it could easily have finished 6-6 or even 7-7.

Burnside (from Jackson's pass) and Allen (from Burnside's lay-off) fired Albion into a 2-0 lead inside the first eighteen minutes, but City hit back immediately through Hannah, after Denis Law had sold Chuck Drury a dummy, only for Kevan to make it 3-1 sixty seconds later with a stinging left-footer.

In the thirty-fifth minute of this ding-dong contest, Joe Hayes scored again for City after Albion's 'keeper Ray Potter had saved superbly from Law, and before half-time further goals by Kevan (forty minutes) and Colin Barlow (forty-four) made it 4-3 in Albion's favour.

On fifty-seven minutes, Allen struck home his second of the afternoon (following some intelligent play by Burnside, Robson and Jackson) and, after Kevan had been denied a third goal (wrongly disallowed for offside) and Law had seen a shot saved by Potter and another hit the bar, Allen duly completed the last of his seven hat-tricks for Albion two minutes from time, when he converted Burnside's deft back-heel pass from 8 yards. City's 'keeper Bert Trautmann, despite conceding six goals, had a fine game, producing superb saves to deny Allen and Robson. This was Albion's fourth successive home win over City.

Allen bagged his last Albion hat-trick
on 24 September 1960.

Wolves Gobbled Up Again

Wolverhampton Wanderers 1 Albion 5
League Division 1, 28 March 1962, Att. 20,558

This was Albion's second win on Wolves soil in two months, following their FA Cup triumph in January. And what a tremendous one it was.

Robson set the ball rolling inside ten minutes with an accurate shot past Malcolm Finlayson.

Baggies 'keeper Tony Millington then saved well from Terry Wharton before England star Peter Broadbent, against the run of play, netted a lucky equaliser shortly on the half-hour mark.

Just before the interval, Albion regained the lead when Chuck Drury scored his only goal for the club with a scorching volley from distance.

Broadbent came close again for Wolves, as did Kevan and Robson at the other end before Keith Smith, in acres of space, cracked in a third for Albion in the fifty-seventh minute.

With Wolves offering nothing, Kevan netted with a full-blooded header from Alec Jackson's sublime cross in the seventieth minute to make it 4-1 and right at the death Bobby Thomson, later playing for England, who had made his Wolves debut against Albion in the earlier cup tie, turned Jackson's cross into his own net to seal the Baggies' biggest win at Molineux since 1893. And it was a result they would repeat fifty years later.

Four-Goal Hero

Albion 7 Blackpool 1
League Division 1, 28 April 1962, Att. 17,463

Before this superb victory, Albion skipper Don Howe was presented with the Midland Footballer of the Year award, but it was his international teammate Kevan who stole the show with four cracking goals.

It took the beefy striker just thirty seconds to get going when he blasted in Jackson's lay-off with only his second touch of the game. Seven minutes later, the Yorkshireman swept the ball

Bobby Hope's skills ripped Blackpool to shreds.

home from close range after Bobby Hope had freed Clive Clark and followed up with his third goal from Jack Lovatt's splendid pass in the twenty-fifth minute.

After Ray Charnley had pulled one back for the Seasiders just before half-time, Lovatt slipped in Albion's fourth goal on fifty-two minutes; Robson made it five with a quarter of an hour remaining; Howe scored a sixth from the penalty spot and finally Kevan smashed in Albion's seventh three minutes from time, to bring his overall total for the season to thirty-four – this after he had been named as reserve in England's World Cup squad for Chile.

And Four More for Kevan

Albion 6 Fulham 1
League Division 1, 8 September 1962, Att. 19,304

Fulham, without former Albion star Robson, Johnny Haynes and Alan Mullery among others, were effectively reduced to ten men when Graham Leggatt was injured on eleven minutes. But despite their problems, the visitors took the lead on nineteen minutes when Jackie Henderson fired past Tony Millington.

However, after that setback, it was a case of how many goals Albion would score!

They managed six with Kevan bagging his second four-timer in seven games.

The striker equalised with a thumping header on twenty-one minutes; Keith Smith followed up his first effort to net a second goal two minutes later and the same player made it 3-1 in the thirty-eighth minute after Tony Macedo had saved Kevan's low shot.

Early in the second half, Kevan glided home Bobby Cram's right-wing cross for 4-1 and just before the hour mark, Albion's in-form goal machine lunged forward to convert Alec Jackson's measured centre.

Finally, in the sixty-ninth minute, England World Cup winner George Cohen gifted Kevan his fourth goal and Albion's sixth with an error inside his own penalty area.

The half-dozen goals scored by the Baggies made it twelve in four home games against Fulham and they would follow up with another sixteen in the next four.

Kev's Fond Farewell

Albion 6 Ipswich Town 1
League Division 1, 9 March 1963, Att. 10,759

Playing his last game for Albion before his £50,000 transfer to Chelsea, Kevan bid farewell to the fans with another hat-trick, although his three goals went past stand-in 'keeper Ted Phillips after Wilf Hall had left the field with a shoulder injury as early as the fourteenth minute.

The Ripon-born striker opened his account on twenty-one minutes, only for future Albion forward Ray Crawford to equalise fourteen minutes later. After that it was, effectively, all Albion.

Kevan made it 2-1 sixty seconds before the interval; Jackson converted Clark's pass for 3-1 on fifty-three minutes and Clark himself weighed in with a fourth halfway through the half.

With thirteen minutes remaining, and Ipswich down to nine men following Doug Moran's injury, Smith fired in Albion's fifth goal before Kevan banged in number six with eight minutes remaining. What a way to say goodbye!

Far left: Ronnie Fenton, who opened the scoring in the Manchester City game.

Left: Winger Kenny Foggo was on song against the Potters in September 1964.

Magic Midget Men

Manchester City 1 Albion 5
League Division 1, 27 April 1963, Att. 14,995

Albion, fielding one of the smallest forward lines in the club's history (average height 5 foot 7 inches), won this relegation encounter in some style.

Left-winger Clark gave City's full-back Bobby Kennedy a torrid afternoon, scored once himself and had a hand in four of Albion's goals.

After a couple of near misses, Ronnie Fenton opened the scoring for Albion on nine minutes. And with three more goals following in the next quarter of an hour, first from Scotsman Kenny Foggo, then a delicate lob by the impetuous Clark and Foggo again, the Baggies were firmly in control at half-time, leading 4-0.

Alex Harley clawed one back for City, but in the very last minute – having twice gone close to scoring earlier – Jackson robbed Cliff Sear to pop in Albion's fifth to clinch their best League win at Maine Road for almost thirty years.

Bobby 'Crams' in Three

Albion 5 Stoke City 3
League Division 1, 12 September 1964, Att. 24,505

By scoring three goals against the Potters, full-back Bobby Cram become the first Albion defender to claim a hat-trick at competitive level since centre-half Sid Bowser netted three times against Bradford City in September 1919.

Trailing to a John Ritchie strike on nine minutes, Baggies right-winger Foggo equalised halfway through the first half, crashing the ball high into the net following a wonderful run by his opposite flanker Clark.

Two minutes later, Cram netted his first goal with a powerful shot, which deflected off Eric Skeels and looped over stranded goalkeeper Lawrie Leslie.

Stoke, however, were back level inside a minute when former Manchester United star Dennis Viollet capitalised on a weak back-pass by Terry Simpson to score with ease. The visitors then stunned the home fans by taking the lead five minutes into the second half, when Ritchie netted from Calvin Palmer's right-wing cross.

Albion equalised again, courtesy of superstar Cram, on fifty-seven minutes. As Clark shimmied into the box, he was bowled over by Alan Bloor, allowing the Albion full-back to step up and ram home the resultant penalty to make it 3-3.

Soon afterwards, Cram was handed another spot-kick when the unlucky Bloor handled a cross from Clark. This time the full-back's straight shot was saved by Leslie, but the Albion defender reacted quickest to bang in the rebound.

Victory was assured for the Baggies when Tony Brown got on the end of Hope's inch-perfect lob to head home his side's fifth goal with twenty minutes remaining.

Late on, Albion 'keeper Potter turned Keith Bebbington's shot round a post while George Kinnell cleared Clark's shot off the line.

The King is Crowned
Albion 5 Wolverhampton Wanderers 1
League Division 1, 10 October 1964, Att. 23,006

Albion's £25,000 signing from Notts County, Jeff Astle, crowned his home debut with a twenty-fifth-minute opening goal to set Albion on their way to a resounding victory over their Black Country rivals.

Wolves 'keeper Fred Davies failed to deal with Hope's cross and as the ball fell, John Kaye (replacing the injured and former 'Wolf' Crawford) laid it off for Astle to fire home.

Eleven minutes after the break, Astle netted again, this time from Clark's smart pull back after the winger had raced past George Showell. On the hour mark, the industrious Kaye, with his head swathed in bandages following an aerial clash just before half-time, whipped in a third goal and he followed up soon afterwards with his second and Albion's fourth, as Wolves seemed to give up!

Peter Knowles, now a Jehovah's Witness, did reduce the arrears on seventy-three minutes, but when 'Man of the Match' Clark was fouled by Showell, Cram stepped up to ram the spot-kick past Davies to clinch an excellent victory.

This was Albion's best home win over Wolves since December 1929.

City Goes to Pot!
Albion 6 Stoke City 2
League Division 1, 18 September 1965, Att. 24,374

Twelve months previous, an eight-goal thriller had ended Albion 5 Stoke 3, and it was Albion again who took the honours, this time with a goal difference of four.

After a quiet opening when neither goalkeeper was tested, Albion took the lead on eighteen minutes when former Baggies player Setters scored an own-goal. Kaye then headed a brilliant second before Cram, a hat-trick hero a year before, made it 3-0 from the penalty spot, conceded by the unfortunate Setters.

Welsh international Vernon pulled a goal back for Stoke on forty minutes, but four minutes into the second half Brown netted Albion's fourth, which was followed soon afterwards by a fifth from the head of Kaye.

Peter Dobing reduced the deficit on the hour, only for Kaye to complete the scoring with his hat-trick goal from Brown's 15-yard pass in the seventy-second minute.

Best Win for a Decade
Albion 8 Burnley 1
League Division 1, 11 November 1967, Att. 18,952

A disappointing crowd witnessed Albion's biggest home League win for ten years, and only two great saves by the Burnley goalkeeper and a 'blind' referee, who missed at least two clear-cut penalties, prevented the Baggies from reaching double figures.

Albion's Scottish Under-23 schemer Hope opened the scoring from long range on sixteen minutes. Clark, who teased and tormented full-back John Angus all afternoon, netted with a brave diving header four minutes later and halfway through the half Brown clipped in a third.

Kaye, with plenty of space, jabbed home Albion's fourth on thirty-five minutes and, right on half-time, defender Eddie Colquhoun sent in a cracker from 20 yards for goal number five.

Hope's second followed in the fifty-ninth minute and another smart header from Clark made it 7-0 as Burnley crumbled! Astle finally got the goal he deserved in the seventy-fifth minute, from Kaye's pass, before Arthur Bellamy grabbed a late consolation for the outclassed and outplayed visitors.

This was Albion's first home win over Burnley in ten starts since 1958 and they have not been able to match this 8-1 triumph since, which remains as the club's third-biggest League victory at The Hawthorns. This was also the Clarets heaviest post-Second World War defeat.

A Boxing Day Treat
Albion 3 Manchester City 2
League Division 1, 26 December 1967, Att. 44,897

Watched by the biggest Hawthorns' League crowd since April 1959, Albion produced one of their best home displays for months by beating the subsequent League champions in a cracking game of football.

Dick Krzywicki was outstanding on the wing in both wins over the League champions-elect.

One expected a few goals with the top two scoring teams in the First Division meeting each other – and the fans weren't disappointed.

City, without Colin Bell, started brightly, Francis Lee and Mike Summerbee both firing wide. Albion's first chance fell to Clark but his shot was too close to goalkeeper Ken Mulhearn.

Albion upped the pace and took the lead on twenty-seven minutes, Astle scoring with a copybook header from Hope's corner-kick.

Ten minutes later, after some excellent interplay involving Hope and Dick Krzywicki, Tony Brown volleyed in a second to put Albion in the driving seat.

After some stern dressing room words by manager Joe Mercer, City came out for the second half full of commitment and after two near misses, Lee, unmarked, scored with a stunning 30-yard angled shot on the hour to reduce the deficit.

All of a sudden the game had swung City's way, and thirteen minutes later the visitors were level when Summerbee thumped home an equaliser as Albion's defence got caught out by a counter-attack. Stan Bowles and Neil Young then had shots saved by Baggies 'keeper John Osborne but a shrewd tactical change, made by manager Alan Ashman, proved crucial.

Graham Lovett, returning to first-team action after breaking his neck in a car crash, had replaced the limping Clark in the seventieth minute, and it was he who kept Albion going forward. The raven-haired midfielder struck the woodwork with a terrific drive, had another shot blocked and set up Brown who missed, before assisting in the build-up which led to Astle's dramatic last-gasp winner.

Lovett, collecting the ball in midfield, fed Brown. He quickly slipped a pass forward to Astle, who charged between two City defenders before smacking home the winner from just inside the penalty area.

City's eleven-match unbeaten run had been terminated by a very efficient Albion side that tackled first and asked questions later!

Twenty-four hours later, Albion won 2-0 at Maine Road to complete the double, their tenth over City since the clubs first met in 1899/1900. City went on to win the First Division title this season while Albion lifted the FA Cup.

Astle Stars in Super Show
Albion 6 Manchester United 3
League Division 1, 29 April 1968, Att. 45,992

Albion had qualified for the FA Cup final forty-eight hours earlier by beating Birmingham City 2-0, while Manchester United was chasing the League and European Cup double.

The gates were closed at The Hawthorns, with 5,000 locked outside. Those present saw Albion start confidently, Astle giving them the lead after just nine minutes following a mistake by Tony Dunn. It was end-to-end action thereafter, but the huge crowd had to wait until the thirty-ninth minute before Ronnie Rees scored Albion's second goal.

After two near misses, Tony Brown converted a twice-taken penalty (conceded by Nobby Stiles on Rees) in the fifty-fifth minute to make it 3-0 and three minutes later Astle swooped to head in number four from Hope's cross.

Stunned United were themselves awarded a penalty when Doug Fraser brought down Brian Kidd and Law scored from the spot. But Albion powered on and netted twice more midway

Jeff Astle (9) scored five goals for Albion in successive home League games over Manchester United in April and August 1968. Albion beat the Reds 6-3 and 3-1.

through the half, Asa Hartford tucking home Astle's nod down from Brown's centre before Astle completed his second hat-trick in three days with a stooping header from Lovett's cross.

United rallied late on and after Law had missed three sitters, Kidd netted twice to make the scoreline look more respectable. United went on to win the European Cup and Albion the FA Cup final, both at Wembley.

City Hit for Six
Albion 6 Coventry City 1
League Division 1, 9 October 1968, Att. 29,255

Producing a ruthless, direct and determined performance, man for man, Albion completely destroyed Coventry's pride and all their early season buoyancy with this impressive victory, and it made one wonder why the Baggies had lost three times in a row to the Sky Blues during the previous twelve months.

Speedy in attack, Albion got off to a cracking start when former City winger Rees slipped inside Dietmar Bruck, collected Ian Collard's pass and drilled the ball low past 'keeper Bill Glazier.

Coventry, sadly lacking in midfield, were over-run at times and it took four first-class saves by Glazier to keep the score down to one.

Always in charge, Albion shot out of the blocks at the start of the second half and on fifty minutes Brown made it 2-0 from the penalty spot after Astle had been bundled to the ground by Brian Hill.

Right: 'Bomber' Brown.

Far right: Asa Hartford ran rings around City at times, October 1968.

Five minutes later, the never-happy George Curtis only half-cleared a Rees cross and Astle swooped to crash home a left-footed volley from 12 yards.

Coventry fought back doggedly and reduced the arrears when Ernie Hunt nodded in Dave Clements' cross, but within minutes, Hartford turned brilliantly inside the box to shoot low into the net to increase Albion's lead to 4-1. That became 5-1 in the seventy-fifth minute when Astle made John Tudor pay for his mistake by lashing the ball home from the edge of the area, and four minutes later when the tenacious Brown crossed hard across the face of goal, the ball struck Tudor in the chest and flew past Glazier.

This was Coventry's heaviest defeat in First Division football at the time and some ten years later, Albion would again thrash the Sky Blues, this time by 7-1, also at The Hawthorns.

United Bombed
Albion 4 Manchester United 3
League Division 1, 6 March 1971, Att. 41,134

This was a real ding-dong, end-to-end seven-goal thriller.

After Albion winger George McVitie had volleyed a good chance over the top, United took the lead when Bobby Charlton's superb pass set up George Best on eighteen minutes. Lovett then cleared off the line from Kidd and Astle had a goal disallowed, before Brown 'bombed' in an equaliser on thirty-two minutes from 15 yards after Alex Stepney had failed to hold a long range shot from Kaye.

A minute into the second half, Baggies 'keeper Jim Cumbes threw long to McVitie who made ground and crossed for Hartford whose shot spun off Paul Edwards, allowing poacher Brown to pick up the pieces from 8 yards (2-1).

Winger John Aston then levelled on fifty-five minutes with a diving header from Willie Morgan's cross, but back came Albion and just before the hour mark, Brown completed his hat-trick when he chased a long clearance, rounded Tony Dunn and cracked the ball high past Stepney. It was action all the way, and once again United drew level when Kidd equalised on sixty-two minutes. But it was gallant Albion who took the points when McVitie crossed from the right for skipper John Wile to plant a towering header past Stepney in the very last minute to end a great game of football.

Battle of Elland Road

Leeds United 1 Albion 2
League Division 1, 17 April 1971, Att. 36,812

This was Albion's first away League win in twenty-eight matches, since their 1-0 success at Ipswich in December 1969. Defeat for Leeds effectively ended their hopes of lifting the title. That honour went to Arsenal by a point (65-64).

This victory at Elland Road hinged on a controversial decision made by referee Ray Tinkler and his linesman.

Leeds were on the attack when the ball was cleared from the Albion penalty area towards the halfway line where Brown was hovering. However, Colin Suggett was ahead of 'Bomber' in an offside position. The linesman ignored Leeds' appeals and allowed play to continue. Brown controlled the ball, ran on unchallenged and squared the ball to Astle, who, himself looking offside, tapped home to put Albion 2-0 ahead. There was a mini pitch invasion by irate Leeds fans but stewards and police intervened, the game continued, and Albion ran out deserving winners, against all the odds.

Albion certainly played well, defending in numbers and limiting Leeds to only a handful of clear-cut chances.

Brown gave Albion an early lead and, in fact, they should have scored twice more before the controversial incident. Allan Clarke sniffed a late goal for Leeds whose boss Don Revie wasn't a happy chappie at the final whistle, unlike his Albion counterpart, Alan Ashman, who was chuffed to bits!

Following the crowd trouble during this match, Leeds were penalised by the FA and were made to play their first four home games of 1971/72 on neutral grounds.

Programme cover for Leeds *v.* Albion, 1971.

Brown Chops Down Forest
Nottingham Forest 1 Albion 4
League Division 2, 12 January 1974, Att. 15,301

Seven days before this game, Tony Brown had scored a hat-trick in Albion's 4-0 FA Cup win over Notts County. This time he whacked in a four-timer as the other Nottingham club, Forest, were comprehensively felled!

Albion had been struggling up front, having netted only thirty-nine goals in their previous fifty League games, but against Forest they – or rather Brown – went to town!

'Bomber' struck as early as the tenth minute, tapping in from 4 yards after a mix-up between goalkeeper Jim Barron and full-back Peter Hindley.

After Baggies 'keeper Peter Latchford had saved from Ian Bowyer, Forest drew level when Duncan McKenzie lashed home from the edge of the area.

This re-ignited Albion's flame and after Forest midfielder Martin O'Neill had a goal disallowed, Dave Shaw dummied for Brown to score from 10 yards, nine minutes before half-time.

It was 3-1 sixty seconds after the break, when a smart move involving Willie Johnston, Len Cantello, Asa Hartford and Allan Glover ended with Brown netting a ricochet off Shaw from close range.

On sixty-four minutes it was game over when Brown, collecting Shaw's square pass, moved forward, rounded Barron and netted with ease. Soon afterwards, Brown shot wide and, almost on time, Shaw's goal-bound shot was saved by Barron.

The last Albion player to score four goals in a game was Derek Kevan *v.* Fulham in 1962 and not since Ike Clarke at Newport in 1946 had anyone netted four on the road.

Century Winners
Aston Villa 1 Albion 3
League Division 2, 2 March 1974, Att. 37,323

This was the 100th League meeting between Aston Villa and Albion and victory for the Baggies was thoroughly deserved.

Left-back Ray Wilson and striker Shaw returned for Albion and Alan Merrick came in for the suspended Hartford. It was Shaw who had the first shot of the afternoon, firing straight at former Baggies' goalkeeper Jim Cumbes.

After some tentative play with defences dominating, Albion's centre-half Wile opened the scoring on twenty minutes with a powerful header into the bottom corner of the Villa net from Glover's wonderfully flighted left-wing corner.

Chris Nicholl had a chance to equalise almost immediately, but failed to control the ball when under pressure from Merrick before Albion scored again on twenty-five minutes.

Long-serving Villa left-back Charlie Aitken handled Astle's downward header, aimed from Tony Brown, giving referee Don Biddle no option than to award a penalty. Despite the attraction of the home fans at the Holte End, Brown banged the spot-kick past Cumbes.

Back came Villa, and within sixty seconds Sammy Morgan had reduced the arrears with a tap-in after some slack marking by Ally Robertson and Wile.

Two minutes later, Albion netted a third goal. Cantello burst down the right and crossed chest high into the danger zone. The ball deflected into space off Ian Ross and quickest to react was 'Bomber' Brown, who lunged forward to bravely head home his fourth goal of the season against the 'old enemy'.

Baggies 'keeper Peter Latchford denied Ray Graydon with a superb one-handed save, while Cumbes clawed away a header from Merrick. Right at the death, Villa's midfielder Chico Hamilton had a 'goal' ruled out for offside.

The attendance was by far Villa's best of the season.

Up, Up and Away
Oldham Athletic 0 Albion 1
League Division 2, 24 April 1976, Att. 22,356

Albion had to win this, their final game of the season, to gain promotion to the First Division.

Over 15,000 fans travelled to Boundary Park, boosting the attendance to over 22,000, and although the game wasn't a classic, it was certainly tense and nerve-wracking.

Albion had chances in the first half, yet nothing clear cut, but after player-manager Johnny Giles' stern pep talk in the dressing room and on hearing news that their nearest challengers Bolton, who could over take them if they lost to Oldham, were leading at Charlton, the players came out with all guns blazing at the start of the second period.

It was still nail-biting stuff, but then on fifty-four minutes, Boundary Park erupted as Tony Brown volleyed Albion in front following some terrific work involving his namesake Ally, Paddy Mulligan and Mick Martin.

Although playing confidently, Albion knew that one mistake could prove fatal. In fact, ex-Baggie Dave Shaw threatened on a couple of occasions before the final whistle sounded to trigger off wild celebrations on the terraces and in the stands, which continued down the M6 and into the early hours of the next day!

For the record, Bolton won 4-0 at Charlton!

Willie the Wing Wizard
Albion 4 Tottenham Hotspur 2
League Division 1, 2 October 1976, Att. 23,461

Though 2-0 down at half-time, Albion stormed back after the break to record a fine win against lowly Spurs.

On thirty-five minutes, Wile's booted clearance hit Chris Jones in the chest and with Albion's defence all at sea, the ball fell nicely for the Spurs' striker to drive home. Three minutes later, debutant winger Peter Taylor capitalised on Cantello's miskick to put the visitors in control.

However, after the break it was a completely different game altogether as Albion, inspired by Scottish international winger Johnston, ripped Spurs apart with some brilliant attacking football.

Tony Brown reduced the deficit with a penalty on fifty-two minutes after Spurs defender Michael Stead decided to 'catch' the ball inside the area. Martin equalised with a deft header from Cantello's cross just past the hour mark; Ray Treacy, back at The Hawthorns for a second spell, added a third on sixty-six, after Pat Jennings had saved at Martin's feet, and two minutes from time, the Irish midfielder rounded things off with his second goal after some excellent work by substitute Joe Mayo and Brown. Don't ever mention this game to Spurs full-back Terry Naylor, who was given a torrid afternoon by Johnston.

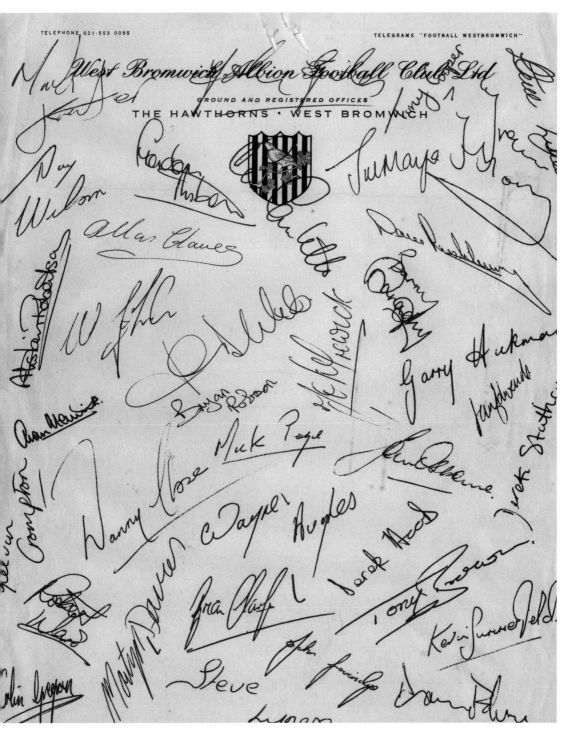

Sheet of autographs from 1976/77 season.

Five-Star Show by Giles & Co

Leicester City 0 Albion 5
League Division 1, 7 May 1977, Att. 18,139

Albion simply outclassed Leicester with a scintillating display of attacking football to register their first win in six games. Master-minded by player-manager Giles who hardly put a foot or a pass wrong, the Baggies were superb at times.

With England's new golden boy, Laurie Cunningham – a £110,000 signing from Leyton Orient who had just won his first Under-21 cap – tearing the home defence to shreds and Martin and Giles winning virtually every tackle in midfield, it was a case of how many goals Albion would score.

Giles controlled the pace from the start, scraping the bar with delicate 25-yard chip after only six minutes.

The floodgates opened seven minutes later when Martin stabbed the ball home after 'keeper Mark Wallington could only parry Tony Brown's long-range shot. But despite Albion's continuous pressure, it was another twenty minutes before they scored again, David Cross soaring above Wallington to glance in Brown's left-wing cross.

The magical skills of Cunningham then produced the best goal of the game. He darted in from the wing, skipped past Steve Whitworth and Brian Alderson before sending a ferocious drive into the roof of the net from 20 yards. It was a brilliant goal.

Leicester, now a spent force, conceded again four minutes after the break when Martin slotted home Cunningham's pass and to round things off, and put the icing on the cake, Brown headed a fifth.

Leicester simply couldn't match Albion for skill and on reflection the score-line could well have been six, seven, or even 8-0.

This was the Baggies' fourth win in five trips to Filbert Street and the 5-0 victory remains to this day, as their best on City soil.

Mick Martin was superb against the Foxes.

Red Faces For United

Albion 4 Manchester United 0
League Division 1, 22 October 1977, Att. 27,526

Having beaten United 4-0 twelve months earlier, Albion once again outfought, outwitted and outplayed the FA Cup holders to record another splendid victory.

Unbeaten in their previous eight home games against United, Albion started well and after two near misses, David Cross opened the scoring on twenty-seven minutes, firing in the rebound after his initial effort had been blocked by 'keeper Stepney.

Wile, always a threat at set pieces, headed in a second from Johnston's corner nine minutes later and shortly before half-time Cross added a third after Derek Statham's shot had bounced off Martin Buchan.

Albion's fourth goal on fifty-six minutes was scored by 'Man of the Match' Cunningham, who stole in at the far post to meet Mulligan's teasing centre.

City in Chocolate Meltdown

Albion 7 Coventry City 1
League Division 1, 21 October 1978, Att. 27,409

A poor Coventry team, wearing a horrid chocolate-coloured strip, were well and truly 'licked' by a more skilful and confident unit.

Albion played very well and, in truth, they would have given any team in the country a run for their money as they made City look a very ordinary outfit!

After the game City boss Gordon Milne said his players were an 'utter disgrace'.

With left-back Statham charging up and down the wing like a greyhound, Cyrille Regis and Tony Brown proving a huge handful through the middle and Cunningham and Cantello creating openings at will, Ron Atkinson's 'Bionic Baggies' were unstoppable.

Cantello opened the scoring on fourteen minutes with a power-drive from Brown's pass. The impressive Cunningham swept in Brendon Batson's centre for number two a quarter of an hour later and Regis headed a third soon afterwards, after some delightful build-up play involving Cantello and Brown.

With Albion totally in charge, Cunningham scored a fourth on sixty-two minutes, sweeping in Wile's flick-on from Brown's corner. City's goalkeeper Les Sealey made several fine saves, one a real stunner from a Regis thunderbolt, before Mick Ferguson surprisingly pulled a goal back for Coventry on seventy minutes – completely against the run of play. But Albion came again and Bryan Robson set up Brown to rifle home a fifth from close range on seventy-six minutes; Regis charged through a static City defence to find the net on eighty-two minutes for number six and Statham rounded things off with a seventh goal on eighty-six, after Terry Yorath had lost possession.

This remains as Albion's best-ever League win over Coventry, and later in the season, by winning 3-1 at Highfield Road, the Baggies recorded their first-ever double over the Sky Blues.

Len Cantello started Coventry's meltdown.

Albion Win Game of the Century

Manchester United 3 Albion 5
League Division 1, 30 December 1978, Att. 45,091

Headlined in the press as the 'Game of the Century', this performance by Albion was quite brilliant ... even United legend Bobby Charlton, sitting in the stand, said so!

Having won at Arsenal four days earlier, Albion were beaming in confidence and took the game to United who weren't playing well, having lost their two previous matches by 3-0, but it was the hosts who struck first, Brian Greenhoff dipping in a vicious volley on twenty minutes.

Tony Brown equalised six minutes later (from Cunningham's cross) and on twenty-seven minutes Cantello smashed in a beauty after Regis's clever back-heel to give Albion the lead. This strike was voted 'Goal of the Season' on ATV's Star Soccer show.

However, within sixty seconds, it was level pegging once more when Gordon McQueen headed home Stewart Houston's free-kick. When Sammy McIlroy wormed his way in from the left-hand touchline to edge United in front, it looked as if Albion had thrown it away.

Not so. After the impressive Cantello and future United star Robson had exchanged passes, Tony Brown ran forward to nudge in a second equaliser on the stroke of half-time.

The action continued after the break. United's 'keeper Gary Bailey saved two tremendous drives from Regis before Cunningham raced 60 yards to put Albion 4-3 in front in the seventy-sixth minute. After a hectic goalmouth scramble in Albion's penalty area, the ball was cleared down the right where Ally Brown held it up before setting up Regis for a blockbusting fifth which secured a stunning and deserved victory for Ron Atkinson's impressive side.

This is only the second time Albion had scored five goals at Old Trafford – the first was in an FA Cup replay in 1939.

Right: Ally Brown was at his best against United.

Far right: Cyrille Regis scored a beauty at Old Trafford.

United Hammered Again!
Albion 5 West Ham United 1
League Division 1, 4 May 1985, Att. 8,834

Getting right to the point, Albion 'hammered' the Londoners in this rather one-sided encounter. Early pressure had failed to break down the visitor's defence and, in fact, it was twenty-five minutes before the first goal was scored, Steve Hunt heading in Steve Mackenzie's cross to give Albion a deserved lead.

Although Ray Stewart equalised with a disputed penalty, Albion hit back hard, Mackenzie netting twice in double-quick time. His first goal was a brilliant individual effort, when he went past three defenders, his second after a well-judged run to beat the offside trap.

After continuous Albion pressure, Republic of Ireland midfielder Tony Grealish scored a rare goal to make it 4-1 on seventy-six minutes and Canadian international winger Carl Valentine set up David Cross (back at the club for a second spell) for number five, eight minutes from time.

This was Albion's best home win over the Hammers for sixty years and their first double over the Londoners since 1969/70.

Good Man, Don
Albion 5 Crystal Palace 3
League Division 2, 26 November 1988, Att. 11,054

Don Goodman, a £50,000 capture from Bradford City, was Albion's star performer in this impressive attacking display by Brian Talbot's team.

Although having the lion's share of the play, Albion had to wait until three minutes before half-time before breaking down a stubborn Palace defence, and it was Goodman who did the trick, snapping up a short back-pass to fire past Brian Parkin.

Surprisingly, Bruce Dyer equalised thirty seconds later and the same player had another chance shortly afterwards before Albion clicked into overdrive and scored three times in a little over a quarter-of-an-hour to open up a 4-1 lead.

Firstly, on fifty-nine minutes, the pacy Goodman ran through a flat back four to bag his second goal and twelve minutes later completed his hat-trick with a smart header.

Robert Hopkins tucked away goal number four in the seventy-fourth minute after some smart play by Carlton Palmer and Colin Anderson, and although Gavin Nebbeling and Geoff Thomas got the visitors back into the game at 4-3 (no-one really expected this) Albion's tall South African striker John Paskin added a fifth for the Baggies, before home goalkeeper Stuart Naylor saved Ian Wright's last-minute spot-kick.

Rampant Baggies
Albion 6 Stoke City 0
League Division 2, 18 December 1988, Att. 17,634

Albion jumped up to third spot in the table after this resounding win over their Staffordshire rivals. Lining up against his former club, Albion's player-manager Brian Talbot had an outstanding game, having a hand in three of his side's six goals.

Gary Robson netted Albion's opener after two minutes, and half an hour later the sprightly Goodman rapped in a second. After the interval Stoke, who had future Albion player Tony Ford sent off on sixty-seven minutes, simply wilted under pressure. Paskin scored twice (in the seventieth and seventy-sixth minutes), Goodman netted again on eighty-five and Robson 'popped' home his second just before time.

This remains as Albion's best-ever win over the Potters in terms of goal difference.

Tykes Tormented
Albion 7 Barnsley 0
League Division 2, 11 November 1989, Att. 9,317

This was a walk in the park for Albion who, by trouncing Barnsley, registered their best League win in terms of goal difference, for twenty-two years.

A disappointing crowd saw in-form Goodman score the opening goal on three minutes, glancing home Ford's right-wing cross. Four minutes later, the unmarked Ford used his head to make it 2-0 and after at least six misses, four of them sitters, Goodman, having initially looked 2 yards offside, ran in to tuck away Talbot's brilliant 40-yard pass for number three close to half-time.

With the second half only fifty-four seconds old, the alert Goodman was at it again, completing his hat-trick with a precise lob from another super pass from Talbot. Two minutes later, Kevin Bartlett netted from close range after 'keeper Ian Wardle had only half-stopped Ford's innocuous shot, and in the fifty-fourth minute, the striker thumped in number six from 15 yards after some superb approach play by Goodman and Ford. With Albion in total command and Barnsley looking disinterested, Bernard McNally blasted in number seven from the penalty spot (after Jim Dobbin's handball) – and there was still over half an hour remaining!

But despite dictating the play and hitting the woodwork twice, plus the fact that Barnsley had substitute defender Sean Dunphy sent off on seventy-four minutes following two nasty fouls on

Goodman, Albion could not add to their score. Nevertheless, they were satisfied with seven and moved up to three places in the table.

This was Martyn Bennett's 218th and final senior appearance for Albion, and he almost scored to celebrate the occasion but hit the crossbar instead of the net!

First in the Third

Albion 6 Exeter City 3
League Division 3, 17 August 1991, Att. 12,892

Ultimately, Albion's first-ever Third Division game against their plucky Devon opponents ended in a comfortable victory.

After some tentative play by both teams, Craig Shakespeare's penalty gave the Baggies a thirtieth-minute lead and, despite Mark Cooper surprisingly equalising, Shakespeare fired in another spot-kick to give Albion a narrow half-time lead. Goodman increased the advantage to 3-1 on fifty-two minutes and the same player, unmarked, added a fourth (from a crossbar rebound) two minutes later.

Adrian Foster and Paul Williams then found the net as Albion increased their lead to 6-1 before Exeter struck twice in the latter stages through Steve Moran and Gary Marshall as the home defence sat back!

This was Albion's first-ever League meeting with the Grecians.

Wembley Bound

Albion 2 Swansea City 0 (Albion won 3-2 on aggregate)
League Division 2, play-off semi-final, second leg, 19 May 1993, Att. 26,045

Albion booked a trip to Wembley for the first time in twenty-three years with this hard-earned but deserved victory over their gritty Welsh opponents, in front of a near-capacity crowd at The Hawthorns.

Going into the match a goal behind, having lost the first leg 2-1 in torrential rain at The Vetch Field, Albion knew they had to win by at least 2-0 to clinch the two-legged semi-final on aggregate.

In effect, the own-goal conceded by Swansea's striker Andy McFarlane in the first match three days earlier, was to prove invaluable, to say the least!

Baggies boss Ossie Ardiles was forced to make one change for the return leg, bringing in Gary Strodder in place of Daryl Burgess, who took a hefty knock as he challenged for a high ball inside the penalty area, which led to that vital own-goal!

Roared on by their supporters, Albion attacked from the start and after Bob Taylor had gone close with a header, the striker ran down the left side of the box before delivering the perfect cross, which Andy Hunt nudged over the line as the clock ticked towards the tenth minute.

It was sheer joy for Taylor's strike-partner, who admitted he should have equalised late on in the first match.

That early goal certainly settled the nerves of the players and fans alike. And it got better nine minutes later. Taylor's shot from almost on the bye-line was pushed round a post by Swans 'keeper Roger Freestone and from the short-corner, taken by Kevin Donovan, midfielder Ian Hamilton nipped round two static defenders to smack home a second goal. Great stuff – Albion 3 Swansea 2 – The Hawthorns was rocking to the chants of 'Wembley, Wembley' and 'Boing, Boing'.

Albion dictated the remainder of the half and should have scored again, Paul Raven, Darren Bradley and Taylor all missing the target.

The atmosphere was electric, and after John Cornforth had headed wide for the visitors, the same player should have been sent off for a crude challenge on Taylor. He stayed on, but in the fifty-third minute, Baggies midfielder Micky Mellon walked, shown a second yellow card for a two-footed lunge on Russell Coughlin.

Two minutes later, Raven left the field for treatment, reducing Albion to nine men. It was getting unbearable as McFarlane twice failed with close range headers.

With the patched-up Raven back on the field, it became ten-a-side when Swans substitute and former Albion striker Colin West, on the pitch for just six minutes, was dismissed for stamping on Hamilton.

Taylor and Bradley should have increased Albion's lead and there were more anxious moments around Tony Lange's goal before the final whistle sounded to trigger off celebration for players and fans alike. What a night.

Alas, for his stupidity, Mellon missed the final.

Boing Boing Baggies!
Albion 3 Port Vale 0
League Division 2, play-off final, 30 May 1993, Att. 53,471

This was Albion's first visit to Wembley since 1970 when they lost to Manchester City in the League Cup final, and a record away following of 42,300 cheered them on to a well deserved 3-0 victory over their Staffordshire rivals Port Vale.

Albion had finished four points and a place below the Valiants in the Division Two table, yet started as favourites. However, despite having the lion's share of the play in the first forty-five minutes, they had nothing to show for their efforts. In fact, former Baggies forward Nicky Cross came close to scoring for Vale while Albion's best two chances fell to the usually reliable Taylor and Hunt.

It was frustrating for all concerned, but then, in the fifty-ninth minute, with Albion trying desperately to break down a resilient defence, Vale's centre-half Peter Swan was sent off by referee Roger Milford for bringing down Taylor as he raced towards goal. 'It was a professional foul – he had to go,' said the official after the game.

This was the turning point, and from that moment on, it was all Albion. Pushing more men forward including right-back Nicky Reid, they finally got the goal they desperately wanted on sixty-nine minutes.

Donovan's right-wing corner was headed against the post by Strodder and after 'keeper Paul Musslewhite had flicked the ball up in the air, Hunt jumped highest to send his header into the net.

It was 'Boing, Boing' on three parts of the stadium, and when Donovan broke clear and laid the ball into the path of Reid to crash home his first goal for the Baggies on eighty-three minutes, it was game over and promotion won for the Baggies!

Late on, Donovan, who had missed three easy chances yet still had a fine match, sealed victory with a third goal from close range after Taylor had won a 50/50 ball with his namesake Ian.

After all the hand shakes and back-slapping, arm-waving and hugging, Albion's delighted skipper Bradley proudly climbed the thirty-nine steps leading to the Royal Box to collect the trophy and, once back on the pitch, said, 'This is the best feeling of my life.'

Albion's winning team at Wembley in 1993 was: Lange in goal; a back four of Reid, Raven, Strodder and Steve Lilwall; a midfield foursome of Donovan, Bradley, Hamilton and McNally and a strike-force of Taylor and Hunt, plus substitute Simon Garner.

Head Wins For Lee
Portsmouth 0 Albion 1
League Division 1, 8 May 1994, Att. 17,629

This was a big, big game for Albion. If they failed to beat Pompey and fellow strugglers Birmingham City won or even drew at Tranmere, then Keith Burkinshaw's team would be relegated after just one season back in Division One. Peterborough and Oxford were already down.

It was certainly a nail-biting climax to a disappointing season, but Albion, backed by 10,000 fans, set about the task in a forthright manner and after a couple of near misses, took the lead on thirty-nine minutes when Lee Ashcroft rose to head home Hamilton's left-wing cross.

A minute later, Taylor shot wide and right on half-time saw another effort saved by 'keeper Alan Knight.

The second period was tense, mighty tense. Albion's 'keeper Lange (deputising for the injured Stuart Naylor) pulled off the save of the season to keep out a curling effort from future Baggies loanee Paul Hall, while Strodder and McNally cleared shots off their own goal line.

At the other end, Donovan, Taylor (twice) and Hunt all came close to increasing Albion's lead, while McNally almost scored with a teasing half volley.

Portsmouth had their moments, Lange dealing well with efforts from Hall and Mark Chamberlain.

With the clock running down, and mobile phones seemingly everywhere, news filtered through that Birmingham had scored a late winner at Tranmere. There was a huge groan from the nervous Albion fans and, I can tell you this for nothing, the last few minutes at Fratton Park were unbearable. But the Baggies held out, and so preserved their status in the League's second tier for another season, at least!

Blues, who amassed the same number of points as Albion (fifty-one) went down on goal difference. Amazingly, Albion finished thirty-nine points behind the champions Crystal Palace this season – but who cared?

Another Tense Finale
Albion 2 Charlton Athletic 0
League Division 1, 7 May 2000, Att. 22,101

This was another nervous end-of-season encounter for Albion and their supporters! Gary Megson's men knew that if they beat newly crowned champions and promoted Charlton, they would retain their First Division status. And they did just that. However, as it happened, a draw would have still kept them up as fellow relegation fighters Walsall lost at Ipswich. In front of the biggest Hawthorns' crowd of the season, Albion had to work hard for the points, and only a superb save by goalkeeper Brian Jensen from future Baggie Mark Kinsella prevented them from falling behind. Also, ex-Albion star Andy Hunt came close for the visitors, who certainly put in some pretty meaty challenges, referee David Pugh showing three Charlton players a yellow card after crunching fouls on Richard Sneekes, Georges Santos and Taylor.

After a goalless first half during which Matt Carbon and Sneekes should have scored, Albion's 'flying Dutchman' finally broke the deadlock in the fifty-fifth minute. Adam Oliver won a free-kick, which was taken by Sneekes, who didn't strike the ball too well. However, it came back to him and with his second attempt fired it low past future Albion 'keeper Dean Kiely, to the relief and joy of the Baggies' supporters. Five minutes after that crucial opening goal – and with Walsall losing at Ipswich – Albion scored a second. Neil Clement charged down the left and crossed perfectly for Taylor to rise majestically to power his header high into the net. Albion were hardly troubled after this and when it was known that the Saddlers had lost at Portman Road, it was celebration time once more in and around the Hawthorns.

It was 1931 over again. Back then it was 'win' to go up; This time it was 'win' to stay up!

Pompey Pompelled

Albion 5 Portsmouth 0
League Division 1, 3 February 2002, Att. 21,028

Generally it seems as though Albion enjoy playing against Portsmouth. In the early 1950s, they twice walloped Pompey 5-0 and also 4-0 at The Hawthorns, as well as winning 6-2 at Fratton Park. And this was another excellent victory.

Playing great football, Albion went in at the break leading 4-0; it could have been six, although Peter Crouch missed a clear chance for the hard-pressed visitors.

Jason Roberts opened the scoring on eight minutes with his fifth goal in eight starts. Neil Clement crossed from the left, Scott Dobie flicked the ball on and the striker was there to fire past Dave Beasant.

Icelander Larus Sigurdsson slipped in his first goal for the club and Albion's second in the twenty-fourth minute, after Dobie's shot had been saved by Beasant. Dobie then made it 3-0 fifteen minutes later from full-back's Igor Balis's miscued cross and, just before the interval, Balis himself bagged a fourth, cutting in from the right to drive the ball over Beasant. This was a terrific goal and his first for the Baggies.

After sustained pressure, when Clement, Roberts and substitute Taylor should all have scored, Roberts ended Pompey's agony with a fifth goal from an acute angle ten minutes from time. This was Albion's biggest win for thirteen years, since beating Barnsley 7-0 in 1989, and victory also earned them their second double over Pompey in successive seasons.

Day of Infamy at the Lane

Sheffield United 0 Albion 3
League Division 1, 16 March 2002, Att. 17,653

This game was abandoned in the eighty-second minute by referee Eddie Wolstenholme after United had been reduced to *six* men – three had been sent off and two taken off, injured! However, after an enquiry, the result was allowed to stand, rightly securing Albion three precious points on their way to promotion.

Blades keeper Simon Tracey was dismissed as early as the eighth minute for handling the ball outside his area. Wilko De Vogt came on and was subsequently beaten by Dobie's fine header in eighteenth minute. After some heated exchanges and a few near misses, Albion went 2-0 up through Derek McInnes on sixty-three minutes. However, within sixty seconds, former

Baggies player substitute Georges Santos, who had been on the pitch barely thirty seconds, was dismissed for a two-footed lunge on Andy Johnson.

Amazingly, just ninety seconds later, United's second substitute Patrick Suffo who hadn't even touched the ball, was shockingly shown a straight red for deliberately headbutting McInnes.

In the seventy-eighth minute, Dobie scored again for Albion after Darren Moore had headed Neil Clements' cross back across goal, but soon afterwards United midfielder Michael Brown was 'taken off for his own good' by manager Neil Warnock.

With Albion in strolling mode against seven men, United's Rob Ullathorne dramatically collapsed on the pitch with a supposed muscle spasm. He went off, leaving the referee no alternative but to abandon proceedings. This was the first time in 114 years of Football League history that a game had to be abandoned due to a 'lack of players.' It was certainly an extraordinary match on an extraordinary afternoon in Yorkshire.

Three Precious Penalty Points
Bradford City 0 Albion 1
League Division 1, 13 April 2002, Att. 20,209

The target was set – Albion needed to win their last two games of 2001/02 to ensure a return to the 'promised land'. This encounter at Valley Parade was the penultimate fixture and it turned out to be a very tense afternoon for the 6,500 Baggies fans who boosted the attendance to over 20,000.

Albion had not won on Bradford's ground since 1906 and in truth they found it tough this time round. Paul Gilchrist and Scott Dobie came closest to scoring in the first half and in fact it wasn't until talisman Bob Taylor was introduced as a seventy-fourth-minute substitute that Albion finally took control of a tight game. After seeing an effort brilliantly saved by 'keeper Alan Combe, the striker should have done better soon afterwards, but shot weakly at goal and then saw Dobie head the rebound over. With time running out, and nervous fans slowly biting their fingernails away, Derek McInnes was pushed over inside the box by Stuart McCall but referee Mike Dean waved play on. Wow – what tension!

Then, in Albion's next attack, Taylor was chopped down by Andy Myers as he went for McInnes' cross. There was no doubt this time as Dean pointed to the spot. After an agonizingly long wait while Taylor was treated for an injury, up stepped right-back Igor Balis to drive in the match-winning penalty in the ninety-fourth minute. A new folk hero was born, and how the fans (and players) celebrated, as the chant of 'We are going up, we are going up' echoed around the whole of Bradford! Victory in their last game at home to Crystal Palace would seal promotion.

Top Flight Baggies
Albion 2 Crystal Palace 0
League Division 1, 21 April 2002, Att. 26,712

This was another tension-packed match and the 2-0 win guaranteed Albion's return to top-flight football for the first time in sixteen years and with it, of course, Premiership football for the first time in the club's history.

Manchester City had already won the title; the second automatic spot was between Albion and Wolves who were away at Sheffield Wednesday.

Cheering their favourites on from the first to the last whistle on an emotional afternoon, the fans witnessed some tentative play, before Albion took the lead on seventeen minutes when Clement's free-kick was headed up by Moore. Danny Dichio challenged two defenders and when the ball dropped down, Moore was there to side-foot home. Sheer relief.

Come half-time, Albion still led 1-0 while at Hillsborough it was 1-1.

Then, on fifty-four minutes, just as Wednesday took the lead against Wolves, so Taylor pounced to put Albion 2-0 up after Latvian 'keeper Aleksandrs Kolinko had fumbled another Clement free-kick. Although Wolves scraped a draw against the Owls, the Baggies held on comfortably to earn their place with the elite of English football as their fans celebrated in glorious fashion.

The after-match scenes of joy and delight will remain in the memories of everyone who was present at The Hawthorns that afternoon.

The attendance was the biggest for a League game at The Hawthorns since January 1993.

Albion, Three Down, Win!

West Ham United 3 Albion 4
League Division 1, 8 November 2000, Att. 30,359

Forty-two years earlier, Albion had come back from 3-0 down to earn a point at Upton Park. This time, having once again found themselves three behind, they went one better and won the game.

The Londoners took the lead after just forty-four seconds. Jermain Defoe slipped past two half-hearted challenges before shooting at goal, the ball deflecting off Thomas Gaardsoe on its way past 'keeper Russell Hoult.

Nine minutes later Brian Deane, after a smart one-two with Don Hutchinson, made it 2-0 and the same player added a third in the eighteenth minute with a back-header from Matthew Etherington's deep free-kick.

After Defoe had missed a sitter, Rob Hulse clawed one back for Albion on twenty-five minutes when Christian Dailly and Michael Carrick got themselves in a right old mess, and five minutes before the break the Baggies' striker netted with a stunning left-footed drive to reduce the deficit to one.

Right on half-time, Defoe was sent off for a reckless challenge of Sean Gregan.

In the sixty-fifth minute, Albion deservedly drew level when Deane diverted Jason Koumas's corner past his own 'keeper. This completed an unusual 'hat-trick' for the former Sheffield United player!

On a high, and with an extra man, Albion powered forward and on seventy-eight minutes substitute Lee Hughes, who had replaced Dobie, scored a dramatic winner. Hammers 'keeper David James failed to get his punch away and Hughes was on hand to hook the ball into the net via Thomas Repka.

There was even time for Hulse to have his 'hat-trick goal' disallowed and miss a sitter, while Albion's Paul Robinson was certainly brought down inside the box.

This was one hell of a comeback and 1,500 Baggies' fans were there to see it! The last time Albion had turned round a three-goal deficit in a League game was in 1893, when they won 4-3 at Nottingham Forest.

Rob Earns His Corn

Charlton Athletic 1 Albion 4
Premiership, 19 March 2005, Att. 27,104

Geoff Horsfield gave Albion the lead at The Valley in the ninth minute, but it was his co-striker Rob Earnshaw who went on to capture the headlines with a wonderfully executed fifteen-minute hat-trick, the first by an Albion in the Premiership.

After making a bright and confident start, Albion were pegged back by Jonatan Johansson's equaliser on twenty-four minutes and although Charlton had defender Tahar El Karkouri red-carded, they had more of the play – that is until Earnshaw arrived on the scene!

In the seventy-third minute, the Welsh international netted with a jack-knife header after a knock-down by Horsfield. In the eighty-fourth minute he collected Zoltan Gera's brilliant 40-yard pass to fire past future Albion 'keeper Dean Kiely, and in the eighty-eighth minute he coolly slotted home from the penalty spot after Richard Chaplow had been fouled. This was also Albion's first away win in the Premiership and their best in the top flight since they beat Leicester 5-0 in 1977.

The Great Escape

Albion 2 Portsmouth 0
Premiership, 15 May 2005, Att. 27,751

Albion, lodged at the foot of the Premiership with thirty-one points, had to win this, their last match of the campaign, and hope that Norwich City (on thirty-three points), Southampton (thirty-two) and Crystal Palace (thirty-two) all slipped up, to retain their top-flight status.

A near capacity crowd – the biggest in the League for twelve years – packed into The Hawthorns to see if Bryan Robson's charges could create history by becoming the first team to avoid relegation having been bottom of the Premiership at Christmas.

The team had been in a similar position eleven years earlier, needing to beat Portsmouth on the final day of the season to stay in the First Division.

Not only were the fans nervous, so too were the players, and early on Baggies striker Earnshaw had a chance but shot wide. The visitors rarely threatened but when they did, Tomas Kuszczak had to be at his best when saving from Aliou Cisse and future Hawthorns star Diomansy Kamara. Before the interval Albion's other front man, Kevin Campbell, missed the target by a yard.

During the interval, news filtered through that both Norwich and Southampton were losing and Palace were winning, and when the second half got underway, Albion seemed to move up a gear, driving forward in numbers, although on the break Pompey looked dangerous, twice forcing Kuszczak into saves.

Then Robson sent on substitute striker Geoff Horsfield for midfielder Jonathan Greening with half an hour remaining, and with virtually his first touch of the ball, the former Birmingham City player scored, firing hard and low under 'keeper Jamie Ashdown at the Brummie Road end of the ground after Zoltan Gera's cross had bounced off the head of defender Dejan Stefanovic. A tremendous roar went up – Albion were on their way. With the pressure seemingly off, on-loan Kieran Richardson added a second goal to secure victory on seventy-five minutes. Everyone waited anxiously for the results to come through and when they did, in Albion's favour, a huge celebration party got underway, on and off the pitch, after what was described universally as the second 'Great Escape.' What a day, what a result, what drama. Those who witnessed it will never forget it.

Toffees Munched Up
Albion 4 Everton 0
Premiership, 19 November 2005, Att. 24,784

On a cold, misty, dank early evening, Albion at last pulled off a decent win in the Premiership, albeit against a rather poor Everton team.

After dominating play for long periods and being denied a fourteenth-minute spot-kick when David Weir certainly handled Jonathan Greening's cross, Albion had to wait until the forty-fifth minute to make the breakthrough, Nathan Ellington coolly stroking home a dubious penalty after he had been tripped 'outside' the area by Tony Hibbert!

Clement made it 2-0 with a fifty-first-minute header from Kamara's well-struck corner and when Nigerian international Kanu squared the ball for Ellington to score on sixty-nine minutes, it was game over at 3-0.

Then, after Baggies defender Curtis Davies had fired wide when it looked easier to score, Rob Earnshaw came on as a substitute to grab the final goal in the last minute after an extraordinarily bad back pass from former Albion star Kevin Kilbane who tried to find his 'keeper (Nigel Martyn) from 50 yards!

With this victory, Albion lifted themselves out of the bottom three, and it was also their best League win over the Merseysiders in forty years, since winning by the same score at The Hawthorns in March 1965.

Phillips' Suffolk Punch
Ipswich Town 1 Albion 5
Championship, 14 October 2006, Att. 22,581

Kevin Phillips scored a hat-trick as Albion recorded their first away win for ten months in front of manager-in-waiting Tony Mowbray, who would take charge at The Hawthorns four days later.

After early pressure from the home side, Albion gradually eased into the game and took the lead through Diomansy Kamara's slick opener on twenty-nine minutes.

Unfortunately, Baggies defender Chris Perry conceded an own-goal seven minutes later, but Ipswich were undone again five minutes before half-time when Phillips flicked home an exquisite free-kick delivered by Jason Koumas.

At the start of the second half, it was evident that the Ipswich defenders were asked to mark 'space' rather than players and Albion capitalised.

In the fifty-fourth minute, a brilliant move involving Koumas and Zoltan Gera ended when the latter's brilliant cross was headed home by Phillips.

Two minutes later it was 4-1 when Kamara raced clear, rounded 'keeper Lewis Price and scored comfortably.

Albion created four more good chances to Ipswich's one, before Phillips rounded things off nicely with a superb individual goal twenty seconds from time. Incoming boss and former Ipswich player Mowbray was delighted with Albion's performance, saying, 'That win was emphatic; it could have been even greater.' It was 164 matches since Ipswich had conceded five goals in a League game.

Champagne Baggies

Middlesbrough 0 Albion 5
League Championship, 19 September 2009, Att. 22,725

This was a champagne performance by table-topping Albion, who extended their unbeaten run to ten matches with an emphatic victory over a poor Middlesbrough team.

Roberto Di Matteo's marauders, firing on all cylinders, won comfortably, the star of the show being former 'Boro academy player Chris Brunt who scored twice in the first half.

After a quiet opening quarter-of-an-hour, Albion picked up the pace and took the lead on seventeen minutes. Rhys Williams fouled Jerome Thomas, allowing Brunt to strike a 25-yard free-kick hard and true, the ball deflecting past wrong-footed goalkeeper Danny Coyne off Baggies' striker Roman Bednar.

Luke Moore and Bednar came close to increasing the lead before Brunt scored again on thirty-one minutes, planting Coyne's hurried clearance back over his head and into the net from 40 yards. Great vision.

A full house at the Hawthorns.

Albion continued to dominate, and three minutes before half-time Graham Dorrans swung over a cross towards Youssef Mulumbu, who netted with a looping header from 8 yards. The home side responded and Sean St Ledger brought a decent save out of Scott Carson. There were further efforts from Dorrans and Brunt before Bednar, taking advantage of leaden, ponderous defending, waltzed in to score a fourth goal from the edge of the box on eighty-two minutes.

Thomas completed the rout in the final minute, with a low shot after outwitting Tony McMahon.

'We've sent out a message to the rest of the League,' said a delighted Di Matteo after seeing Albion record their best away win for thirty-two years, since beating Leicester by the same score in 1977.

Throstles Feather Owls' Nest
Sheffield Wednesday 0 Albion 4
League Championship, 28 November 2009, Att. 20,824

Albion, having scored eleven goals in their previous three matches (all won), completely demolished a poor Wednesday side with some brilliant attacking football.

The game was effectively over by half-time, following two goals by Simon Cox and a third by Jerome Thomas.

As early as the second minute, former Wednesday player Brunt saw his header tipped over by 'keeper Lee Grant and soon afterwards fired a yard wide after Cox had slipped him in.

With Albion in total control, Thomas was booked for diving (inside the area) before Cox struck the opening goal from close range on twenty-three minutes after the home defence had failed to deal with a Graham Dorrans corner.

Seven minutes later, it was 2-0 when Brunt's low cross from the left was touched on by Luke Moore for Cox to score from 10 yards.

Moore then squandered a chance by firing over and full-back Tommy Spurr sent Cox sprawling inside the box before Thomas further increased Albion's lead on thirty-eight minutes with a precise low shot from Cox's pass.

All Wednesday could muster in reply were long-range strikes from Marcus Tudgay and ex-Baggies midfielder James O'Conner, which were comfortably dealt with by Carson.

Albion's pressure was now relentless. Moore, Youssef Mulumbu and Cox all went close while at the other end, a breakaway attack saw Leon Clarke shoot straight at Carson. As it was, Albion had the final say when New Zealander Chris Wood picked out Brunt who fired home from 10 yards for his sixth goal of the season.

It was fifty-seven years since Albion had scored four goals at Hillsborough – in that exciting 5-4 victory on Boxing Day, 1952.

Albion Gun Down Hosts
Arsenal 2 Albion 3
Premiership, 25 September 2010, Att. 60,025

Albion thoroughly deserved this victory, their first on Arsenal soil for twenty-seven years, since Derek Monaghan's single-goal winner at Highbury in 1983.

Playing smooth, attacking yet controlled football, the Baggie matched the Gunners kick for kick in an even first half before going 3-0 up with goals by Peter Odemwingie, Chilean Gonzalo Jara and former Arsenal winger Thomas in the space of twenty-three second-half minutes. Although Samir Nasri scored twice in the last quarter-of-an-hour, Albion's defence held firm to stun the home fans in the 60,000 crowd.

There is no doubt whatsoever that Albion were clearly the better side in the first half, having more possession and creating the better chances. Arsenal simply lacked conviction, whereas Albion looked far more at ease despite seeing both of the Gunners' full-backs Gael Clichy and Bacary Sagna shoot wide, Andrei Arshaven twice hit the post and Nasri fire over.

Albion had their moments, let's not forget that. Odemwingie struck an upright, Brunt sent an effort wide and Thomas missed the target from 10 yards. In fact, it was home 'keeper Manuel Almunia who kept his side in the game, saving Brunt's thirty-seventh-minute penalty after Odemwingie had been brought down by the Spaniard who should have seen 'red'.

Albion deservedly took the lead on fifty minutes. Thomas weaved past Sagna and crossed to the far post where Odemwingie tapped in. Two minutes later, it was 2-0 when Brunt's clever back-heeler nutmegged Clichy, allowing Jara to drive the ball home unchallenged. Wenger brought on three attacking substitutes and went for broke, but Albion's defence stood firm and on seventy-three minutes Thomas was there to turn in Brunt's square pass from the left to put Albion three ahead.

Despite Nasri's late strikes and a flurry of high crosses, Albion weren't to be denied. Three weeks later they drew 2-2 at Old Trafford.

At Last, A Win at Villa Park
Aston Villa 1 Albion 2
Premiership, 22 October 2011, Att. 34,152

After thirty-two years of waiting, Albion finally won a League game at Villa Park. And they deserved it, albeit against ten men!

Having beaten Wolves six days earlier, the Baggies were beaming with confidence going into this, the 135th League meeting between the clubs. And they showed their intent from the start, although chances at both ends were few and far between.

After Villa's right-back Alan Hutton had clattered Long (he received a yellow card which should have been red) the hosts took the lead when Darren Bent converted a twenty-third-minute penalty after being brought down by Albion 'keeper Scott Carson.

Then, in the thirty-sixth minute, came a moment of controversy when assistant referee Darren Cann indicated to referee Phil Dowd that Villa's Chris Herd had stamped on Jonas Olsson inside the penalty area. Herd was sent off, but Chris Brunt blasted the spot-kick wide. However, from that point on, there was only going to be one winner – Albion.

Having looked threatening before, they certainly looked dangerous against ten men and a minute before the interval, Olsson equalised with a firm header from Brunt's corner. Playing confidently, Albion made the extra man count, big time!

In the fifty-seventh minute, another well-taken corner by Brunt fell to Austrian international Paul Scharner, who swivelled smartly before firing the ball high into Shay Given's net. This proved to be the winning goal, although Odemwingie and Brunt came close to adding to the score.

In fact, Albion never looked in danger of losing the game, even drawing it, after they had taken the lead.

Baggies boss Roy Hodgson said afterwards, 'If I've ever seen a challenge that merited a red card, it was Hutton's on Long. It was outrageous!'

Another Long Wait Over
Newcastle United 2 Albion 3
Premiership, 21 December 2011, Att. 51,060

Amid the euphoria of Newcastle's dream start to the season, manager Alan Pardew did warn there would be dark days and nights ahead. How right he was, as Albion, who hadn't won a League game at St James' Park since 1977 when Cunningham and Regis scored in a 3-0 win, gained an impressive victory.

Nigerian international Odemwingie outpaced Fabricio Coloccini to put Albion ahead on twenty minutes. Although Demba Ba equalised from a free-kick fourteen minutes later, sixty seconds before half-time, Brunt's terrific cross was headed down by Paul Scharner to Gareth McAuley who scored from 6 yards.

It was action all the way after the break, and on eighty-one minutes Demba Ba notched his second equaliser for the Geordies. Albion came again, and Shane Long, who had earlier hit the bar, found space before crossing for Odemwingie to set up Scharner for the winner five minutes from time.

Wolves Slaughtered In Their Own Den
Wolverhampton Wanderers 1 Albion 5
Premiership, 12 February 2012, Att. 27,131

Striker Odemwingie was the hero of the hour as he became the first Albion player to score a hat-trick at Molineux since the legendary Ronnie Allen in the FA Charity Shield in 1954. Odemwingie confirmed Albion's first-half dominance with a thirty-fourth-minute opener, only for Steven Fletcher to equalise on the stroke of half-time. Jonas Olsson's clever flick restored Albion's advantage on sixty-four minutes; Odemwingie made it 3-1 with less than a quarter of an hour remaining, and substitute and former Wolves player Keith Andrews celebrated his debut with a fourth goal on eighty-five minutes. Odemwingie then stepped up to net his hat-trick goal to seal Albion's fifth win at Molineux in their last seven visits. It was also their biggest victory over Wolves since 1964, their best at Molineux since 1962, and it completed their tenth double over their arch-rivals in League history. Great stuff.

Gera's Special
Albion 3 Liverpool 0
Premiership, 18 August 2012 , Att. 26,039

Steve Clarke's competitive reign at The Hawthorns got off to a dream start as Albion demolished his former club Liverpool.

Having weathered an early Reds storm, when Luis Suarez should have scored, Zoltan Gera's rocket – his first goal since his return to the club from Fulham - gave the Baggies a deserved half-time lead. It was more of the same after the break before two penalties in the space of four minutes swung the game in the Albion's favour.

The visitors were reduced to ten men in the fifty-ninth minute, when Daniel Agger brought down Shane Long in the box and was red-carded for his troubles. However, the Irish international missed the spot-kick only for Odemwingie to spare his blushes on sixty-three when he hammered home Albion's second penalty after Martin Skrtel had fouled the impressive Long.

On loan debutant from Chelsea, Romelu Lukaku, sealed victory in the seventy-seventh minute with a fine headed goal from Liam Ridgewell's precise cross.

Argentinian midfielder, Claudio Yacob, also made his Albion debut.

This was Albion's biggest top flight opening day win since August 1977 when they beat Chelsea, also by 3-0. As for Liverpool's new boss, Brendan Rogers, it was certainly a baptism of fire. Even Kenny Dalglish's team was not humiliated like this!

Chelsea Get the Blues

Albion 2 Chelsea 1
Premiership, 17 November 2012, Att. 25,933

Albion thoroughly deserved this victory, as Chelsea's worst run under former Baggies manager, Roberto Di Matteo continued. In fact, this was Albion's second successive Premiership win over the Blues, their sixth at home in 2012/13, and it lifted them to the dizzy heights of fourth place.

Long was outstanding throughout, scoring the opener, when he exposed David Luiz's poor positioning to head in Morrison's centre on ten minutes.

The nippy Irishman then set up Albion's second five minutes into the second half for Odemwingie with a superb cross that the Nigerian nodded past Petr Cech – this after Eden Hazard had hauled Chelsea level shortly before the interval with a header from César Azpilicueta's cross. But that was a rare highlight for Chelsea on a day that belonged to Albion, who could easily have doubled, even trebled their goal tally, had it not been for the excellence of Cech. Baggies 'keeper Boaz Myhill produced two fine saves himself from Daniel Sturridge.

Long's performance was all the more impressive because he was playing twenty-four hours after being told that his grandmother had passed away. The striker paid tribute to her by unveiling a message on his T-shirt after scoring that said 'Rest in Peace Nan'. In contrast, Chelsea's striker Fernando Torres once again looked out of sorts.

Strike Trio Bury Saints Alive!

Southampton 0 Albion 3
Premiership, 27 April 2013, Att. 31,946

Backed by more than 3,000 supporters, the majority taking advantage of free coach travel provided by the club, Albion broke their Premiership points record for a season with a competent and stylish victory over Southampton. Marc-Antoine Fortune's second goal of the campaign, a scrambled effort on six minutes, following Graham Dorrans' corner, set the Baggies up for their fourteenth top-flight victory of 2012/13 – another Premier League best. And, in truth, at half-time Albion could, and should, have been four or even five goals to the good! Teenage striker Romelu Lukaku missed three good chances, Shane Long one, and Jonas Olsson should have done better with his header.

Lukaku eventually doubled Albion's lead and took his season's tally to fourteen in the sixty-seventh minute, when he netted comfortably after Fortune had set him up, and ten minutes later he turned supplier as he teed up Long, who himself moved into double figures with a low drive through the legs of 'keeper Artur Boruc.

Unfortunately, there was an ill-tempered finish to the game as Saints' substitute Gaston Ramirez was sent off for elbowing Long, and Fortune quickly followed him down the tunnel for retaliating with a push in the Uruguayan's face.

Things went from bad to worse for the hosts, who were reduced to nine men when Danny Fox was shown a straight red card for a two-footed lunge on Steven Reid.

Referee Robert Madley was in charge of his first Premiership game, and at twenty-seven, he was also the youngest in the top flight.

Victory moved the Baggies up to forty-eight points – one more than they amassed in each of the previous two seasons. It was also their first-ever win at St Mary's and their first the double over Saints since 1969/70.

Lukaku would go on to top Albion's scoring charts in 2012/13 with seventeen goals, including a hat-trick in a thrilling 5-5 draw with champions Manchester United on the final day of the season which was manager Sir Alex Ferguson's 1,500th and last game in charge of the Reds (1986–2013).

THE BEST OF THE REST

29 September 1888   Albion recorded their first home win by beating Burnley 4-3 before 2,100 spectators; Walter Perry, Bassett, Willie Hendry and Charlie Shaw as their goalscorers.

6 October 1888   Albion's biggest 'first season' win was 5-0 against Derby County, Tom Pearson hitting the game's best goal.

4 November 1889   Pearson scored Albion's first League hat-trick – a four-timer in a 6-3 win over Bolton Wanderers.

25 October 1890   Sammy Nicholls had the honour of bagging Albion's 100th League goal, in a 3-2 win at Everton.

8/15 September 1894   All five Albion forwards scored in a 5-1 hammering of Wolves. A week later, Albion beat Liverpool 5-0.

20/27 April 1896   By finishing bottom of the League, Albion competed in the test matches (the equivalent of today's play-offs). They retained their top-flight status by beating Manchester City 6-1 and Liverpool 2-0.

16 September 1899   Ben Garfield had the pleasure of scoring Albion's 500th League goal – in a 2-0 home win over Liverpool.

16 April 1900   Albion won their last game at Stoney Lane in style, thrashing Nottingham Forest 8-0, Billy Walker (three), Dick Roberts (two), Simmons (two) and John Chadburn the scorers.

3 September 1904   Debutant Albert Lewis scored all of Albion's goals in a 4-1 win at Burnley.

26 December 1906   Fred Shinton became first Albion player to score twenty-five League goals in a season, reaching his target in a 3-0 win over Burslem Port Vale.

Far left: Alf Bentley was signed from Bolton for £500.

Left: Charlie Wilson's hat-trick helped Albion beat rivals Birmingham 5-1 on 6 February 1926.

16 February 1907	The first vicar to play for Albion, the Reverend Willie Jordan, scored a hat-trick on his debut in a 5-0 victory over Gainsborough Trinity.
26 December 1907	Buck's hat-trick goal in a 3-1 away win at Barnsley was Albion's 1,000th in the Football League.
26 December 1911	Hubert Pearson became the first Albion goalkeeper to score in a League game, netting a penalty in a 2-0 win over Bury. Later in the season Pearson scored another *v.* Middlesbrough.
10 February 1912	Hat-trick hero Bob Pailor was the star as Albion beat his future club Newcastle 3-1 at The Hawthorns.
6 September 1913	Debutant Alf Bentley, signed from Bolton for £500, scored all of Albion's goals in a 4-1 win over Burnley.
26 December 1919	Almost 44,000 fans saw Albion make it five League wins on the trot with a 4-0 romp over Sunderland.
17 January 1920	Having whipped Blackburn 5-1 at Ewood Park earlier in the month when Bentley netted a hat-trick, Albion repeated the dosage with 5-2 home victory to complete their first double over Rovers since 1897.
10 April 1920	By beating Bradford 3-1, Albion were officially crowned Football League champions for the first time. Jephcott, Bentley and Bowser (penalty) scored the goals which took the team's tally for the season to ninety-nine. Morris netted the 100th against Liverpool a fortnight later.

13 December 1924	George James recorded the fastest-ever goal by an Albion player – netting after just five seconds against Nottingham Forest. James went on to score three more in a 5-1 win.
6 February 1926	'Tug' Wilson (three) and James (two) scored in Albion's 5-1 win over Birmingham – their best victory over Blues at that time.
7/21 January 1928	Cookson became the first Albion player to score four goals in an away game, in a 6-0 win at Grimsby. He bagged four more in the next match (5-3 *v.* Reading) and ended the season with a record thirty-eight.
26 December 1929	W. G. Richardson scored on his Albion debut in a 6-1 win over Millwall. He went on to bag 202 League goals for the club, his last in 1939.
19 April 1930	Albion scored a record 105 goals in 1929/30, Cookson leading the way with thirty-three, including four in a 7-1 win over Hull City.
6 September 1930	Cookson notched his fourth four-timer for Albion in a 6-3 win at Cardiff.
6 October 1934	W. G. Richardson was Albion's four-goal hero in their 6-3 victory over Leeds.
7 December 1935	Having already put four past Grimsby, seven past Aston Villa and five past Sheffield Wednesday, Albion continued to rattle in the goals by beating Everton 6-1. Before the season ended they would score two more fives, a six and an eight.
2 May 1936	By scoring in a 3-1 last game victory over Birmingham, W. G. Richardson broke Cookson's record of thirty-eight goals in a season.
11 March 1939	England star Joe Johnson, signed from Stoke, was the first left-winger to score four goals in a League game for Albion – in a 6-0 win over Bury.
29 April 1939	Only 3,109 fans saw W. G. Richardson score the last of his 202 League goals for Albion in a 4-2 win over Norwich.
5 April 1947	Ike Clarke's last hat-trick for Albion blew away Bury 3-0 in a gale-force wind at The Hawthorns!
17 May 1947	Len Millard scored a terrific goal from 35 yards in Albion's 5-1 win over Nottingham Forest.
24 April 1948	Arthur Rowley scored 434 League goals, more than any other player, four coming with Albion, his last in a 5-0 win at Cardiff.

8/15 September 1948   Goalless in their previous two games, Albion got back on track with a 5-0 win over Lincoln, with Dave Walsh netting a hat-trick. A week later Albion won 3-0 at Sincil Bank to complete the double.

11 December 1948   Cyril Williams scored his only hat-trick for Albion in a 5-2 win over Grimsby. This took Albion's tally of goals against the Mariners to twenty-four in six matches since 1932.

5 November 1949   Walsh scored a stunning goal in Albion's 4-0 win over Everton, whose 'keeper Ted Sagar played brilliantly!

27 October 1951   Level at the break, Albion scored three goals in three second-half minutes to beat Liverpool 5-2, their biggest-ever win at Anfield.

26 December 1951   Ronnie Allen scored his first hat-trick for Albion in a 3-2 win over Bolton.

23 April 1952   Albion won 4-1 at FA Cup finalists Newcastle 4-1, Ryan, Lee, Nicholls and Allen on target. Albion would win 5-3 and 7-3 in their next two visits to St James' Park.

6 April 1953   Allen scored a late penalty as Albion beat Aston Villa 3-2 at The Hawthorns.

10 October 1953   Over 47,000 saw Allen claim another hat-trick as table-toppers Albion beat second-placed Huddersfield 4-0.

24 October 1953   Another Allen hat-trick came in a 5-2 win over Chelsea. Two of his goals, on ten and fifty-three minutes, were crackerjacks following corner-kicks.

25 December 1953   It was Christmas Day cheer for Albion, who beat lowly Liverpool 5-2, Frank Griffin celebrating his 100th appearance for the club with a double. Despite there being no transport facilities, a crowd of over 30,000 turned out to see the Baggies climb back to the top of the table.

2 January 1956   Albion made it nineteen goals in four trips to Newcastle as Allen's treble earned them a 3-0 win.

2 February 1957   Albion, 2-0 down, turned things round at Chelsea to win 4-2, three goals coming in the last seventeen minutes. Unfortunately, Chelsea's 'keeper Reg Matthews went off injured shortly before half-time.

11 October 1958   Behind after thirteen minutes, Albion rallied to win 4-1 to register their best away win over Aston Villa since 1935.

Right: Alec Jackson, the 'Tipton Slasher', scored a hat-trick in Albion's 6-0 win over Newcastle in September 1960.

Far right: England winger Laurie Cunningham.

5 September 1960	Albion, having lost their first five games of the season, clicked into gear and smashed Newcastle 6-0, Alec Jackson scoring his first-ever hat-trick.
18 November 1961	Kevan missed four sitters before scoring a hat-trick as Albion came from behind to beat Sheffield United 3-1.
22 September 1962	In Albion's 5-4 win over Bolton, two players, Kevan and Francis Lee, both scored hat-tricks – the latter's haul included two penalties.
18 October 1963	Albion, two behind after twenty-three minutes, and despite Jackson missing a penalty, hit back to beat Aston Villa 4-3.
31 March 1964	Mickey Fudge, aged eighteen, playing in only his eighth game, scored a hat-trick in Albion's 4-2 win over reigning champions Everton.
26 August 1964	Sunderland, with fifteen-year-old Derek Forster in goal, were outplayed as Tony Brown scored his first Albion hat-trick in a 4-1 win.
27 February 1965	Cram tore a hole in the net with his penalty kick and Astle scored with a superb header as Albion beat Aston Villa 3-1.
13 March 1965	Albion, defeated 4-2 at Leicester earlier in the season when Astle made his debut, gained revenge by winning the return fixture 6-0.

4 September 1965   Twice behind, Albion hit back to beat Sheffield Wednesday 4-2. Astle's hat-trick included two terrific headers.

10 September 1965   A rare Friday night game saw Albion go to the top of the table with a 4-3 win at newly promoted Northampton, courtesy of Astle's second hat-trick in a week.

10 September 1966   Left-winger Clark starred in Albion's 5-1 win over Fulham. He scored twice, made another and gave England's right-back George Cohen a torrid time.

26 December 1966   With eighteen-year-old full-back Dennis Clarke making his debut and 37,969 fans present, 'Bomber' Brown netted another hat-trick as Albion beat Tottenham 3-0.

13 May 1967   Albion swept Newcastle aside with contemptuous ease to win 6-1, Brown (three), Foggo, Graham Williams and Clark the scorers.

30 September 1967   Astle bagged three hat-tricks in 1967/68 – his first in a comfortable 4-1 home win over Sheffield United.

1 May 1968   A first-half goal by West Ham's Martin Peters was over-powered by Astle's hat-trick in Albion's 3-1 win.

14 August 1968   FA Cup holders Albion beat European champions Manchester United, 3-1 before 38,299 fans. Facing Best, Charlton, Law, Stiles and Co., Astle took his tally of goals against the Reds to five in two games.

19 April 1969   John Kaye's wife presented him with a baby daughter as he scored his first goal of the season in Albion's 5-1 win over Newcastle.

Three for 'Pop' Robson against the
Suffolk Punchers, March 1977.

10 January 1970   Albion trailed twice before bouncing back to beat Crystal Palace 3-2 with yet another Astle hat-trick.

12 December 1970   Kaye was making his 200th appearance for Albion, but it was 'Bomber' Brown who took the plaudits with a hat-trick in a 3-1 win over Spurs.

1 January 1972   Albion, 2-0 down at half-time, staged a magnificent second-half fight-back to win 3-2 at Ipswich, George McVitie netting the winner on eighty-two minutes.

11 April 1973   Albion, battling against relegation, gave themselves hope with a 4-1 win over Everton. Alas, it was all in vain!

16 March 1977   Thumped 7-0 at Portman Road earlier in the season, Albion gained ample revenge with a 4-1 win over Ipswich at The Hawthorns. Bryan Robson scored a hat-trick as Tony Godden and Laurie Cunningham made their home debuts.

15 April 1978   A brilliant twenty-second-minute solo goal by Regis, who glided past Dave Watson and Mick Doyle, set Albion up for a fine win 3-1 win at Manchester City.

30 September 1978   Brown equalled Allen's record of 208 League goals with Albion's clincher in a 3-1 win at Chelsea.

14 October 1978   A fortnight after drawing level with Allen, Brown netted his 209th League goal, a 25-yard belter in a 3-1 win at Leeds.

16 December 1978   Albion recorded their best win at Molineux since 1962 with a comprehensive 3-0 victory over Wolves. Brown netted a superb 25-yarder.

1 January 1979   Albion 'waltzed' into second spot in the First Division with an efficient 3-1 win over Bristol City on The Hawthorns 'skating rink.'

15 September 1979   Albion registered their second successive 4-0 home win over Manchester City, Brown, Kevin Summerfield, Gary Owen (against his former club) and Robson the scorers.

2 February 1980   With a 3-1 win, Albion doubled up over Manchester City for the first time since 1967/68. Peter Barnes netted twice against his former club.

7 February 1981   Goals by Robson and Regis brought Albion their first home victory over the Liverpool (the reigning champions) since 1966.

25 September 1982   A Regis hat-trick saw off Norwich 3-1 at Carrow Road, his last goal came after a classic 'through the middle' charge.

13 October 1984   Albion brilliantly beat Nottingham Forest 4-1, Garry Thompson's hat-trick the stand-out feature.

24 October 1987   Ex-Aston Villa and England winger Tony Morley netted his first hat-trick in English football as Albion pipped Huddersfield 3-2.

15 October 1988   Ron Atkinson's last game as Albion manager resulted in a 4-1 win at Birmingham, whose boss was ex-Baggie Garry Pendrey with Tony Brown his assistant. Blues had Vince Overson sent off on twenty-seven minutes and thereafter it was all Albion, with Robert Hopkins scoring twice against his former club.

8 February 1992   The Blues' biggest home crowd since 1988 – 27,508 – saw Albion win 3-0, their fifth consecutive victory at St Andrew's and their twelfth since 1957.

3 January 1993   Exeter, 2-0 up, had 'keeper Kevin Miller sent off for fouling Bob Taylor, allowing Ian Hamilton to win the match for Albion from the spot (3-2).

3 April 1993   On-loan debutant from Newcastle Andy Hunt scored a hat-trick in seven second-half minutes as Albion beat Brighton 3-1.

5 September 1993   Darren Bradley's sublime goal and Kevin Donovan's clinical finish in the 3-2 win over Wolves.

Canadian international Paul Peschisolido, who scored Albion's first away hat-trick for fifteen years in the 4-2 win at Norwich on 15 January 1997.

26 February 1994	Taylor and Paul Mardon scored in a 2-1 win at Molineux as Albion claimed their first League double over Wolves since 1981/82.
15 March 1995	Four ex-Albion players lined up for Wolves who lost 2-0 at The Hawthorns, Lee Ashcroft and Taylor, with the goal of the season, on target. Albion had lost at Molineux earlier in the season.
22 March 1995	Having crashed 5-2 to Swindon in the previous home game, Albion bounced back to beat Millwall 3-0 with another Hunt treble in front of the season's lowest crowd, just 11,782.
30 April 1995	Ashcroft scored a hat-trick in nine second-half minutes as Albion whipped play-off chasing Tranmere 5-1.
10 September 1996	Just over 13,000 fans saw Hunt bag his third Albion treble in a 3-2 win over Reading.
15 February 1997	Canadian Paul Peschisolido scored Albion's first 'away' hat-trick in fifteen years in a 4-2 victory at Norwich.
24 August 1997	Albion fans voted Wolves defender Keith Curle as their 'Player of the Year' after his own goal gave the Baggies a 1-0 victory at The Hawthorns.
27 September 1997	Unbeaten in twenty-nine home games, Bury were undone by another Peschisolido treble which gave Albion a 3-1 victory.
31 January 1998	Hunt's lone-goal winner against Wolves at Molineux, which sent the travelling Baggies' fans wild with delight.
22 August 1998	Lee Hughes notched his first hat-trick for Albion in a 3-0 win at Port Vale.
3 November 1998	Hotshot Hughes – with a header, a tap-in and a ninety-second-minute penalty – claimed another hat-trick in a 3-2 win over Crystal Palace.
14 November 1998	And it was no stopping Hughes, who continued his goal-charge with another three-timer in Albion's 3-0 win over Huddersfield.
26 October 1999	Enzo Maresca's stunning goal clinched a 2-0 win for Albion at Crystal Palace. The Italian moved to Juventus for £4.5 million three months later.
17 October 2000	Hughes' down-the-middle penalty strike gave Albion a 1-0 derby win over Wolves.

18 November 2000   16,410 fans saw Hughes claim his fourth hat-trick as Albion beat Gillingham 3-1 in the first-ever League meeting between the clubs.

25 November 2000   Yet another treble for 'Ginger Ninja' Hughes, in a 3-1 win over Preston, making it eleven goals in ten games. The striker also became the first Albion player to net a hat-trick in successive League games since Astle in 1968.

8 September 2001   Albion blitzed Kevin Keegan's Manchester City 4-0. Derek McInnes scored from 20 yards and Neil Clement netted with a terrific free-kick.

2 December 2001   Jordao was Albion's match-winner at Wolves (1-0).

23 February 2002   Albion thumped Portsmouth 5-0. Jason Roberts netted twice as the Baggies scored five in the League for the first time since 1996.

31 August 2002   A forty-eighth-minute goal by Darren Moore gave Albion their first-ever Premiership win, 1-0 over Fulham before 25,461 fans.

21 February 2004   Albion's 100th game against Sheffield United resulted in a 2-1 win, with defenders Moore (seventy minutes) and Thomas Gaardsoe (eighty-five) scoring before 24,805 spectators. Moore's own goal had given the Blades a fifty-sixth-minute lead.

3 March 2012   Almost 25,000 fans saw Albion gain their first victory over Chelsea in thirty-three years, with Gareth McAuley's eighty-second-minute goal doing the trick! The Londoners had won the previous thirteen Premiership games against Albion.

22 April 2012   43,660 saw Odemwingie's seventy-fifth-minute goal give Albion their first victory at Liverpool since Astle's winner in 1967.

25 November 2012   Albion registered their biggest win at Sunderland in forty-six years, Marc Antoine-Fortune scored a superb last goal in a 4-2 victory.

ALBION'S LEAGUE FACTS & STATS

Top 10 Scorers

218   Tony Brown
208   Ronnie Allen
202   W. G. Richardson
157   Derek Kevan
145   Joe Carter
137   Jeff Astle
135   Tommy Glidden
113   Bob Taylor
112   Fred Morris
103   Jimmy Cookson

Top 10 Appearance-Makers

574   Tony Brown
506   Ally Robertson
500   John Wile
455   Jesse Pennington
445   Tommy Glidden
436   Len Millard
434   Joe Smith
415   Ronnie Allen
414   Joe Carter
403   Ray Barlow

Biggest League Wins

Home: 12-0 *v.* Darwen, April 1892
Away: 8-0 *v.* Wolves, December 1893

Most Goals in a Game

6   Jimmy Cookson *v.* Blackpool (h,) 17 September 1927
5   Fred Morris *v.* Notts County (h), 19 October 1919
5   Derek Kevan *v.* Everton (h), April 1962

Albion's Records in League Football: 1888 – 2013

Premiership

P	W	D	L	F	A
266	66	67	133	286	431

Football League

P	W	D	L	F	A
4324	1710	1057	1557	7776	6313

Test Matches & Play-offs

P	W	D	L	F	A
12	6	2	4	21	14

All 'League' Games

P	W	D	L	F	A
4602	1782	1126	1694	8083	6758

Baggies' League Records

All of Ronnie Allen's 208 League goals for Albion came in the First Division; he had his best season in 1951/52 with a total of thirty-two.

W. G. Richardson holds the club record for scoring most League goals in a season, netting thirty-nine in 1935/36. He was Albion's leading scorer six seasons running: 1930/31 to 1935/36 inclusive.

Albion's biggest home League attendance – 60,945 – was set against Wolves on 4 March 1950.

Albion's lowest-ever home League attendance of 405 was against Derby County on 29 November 1890.

W. G. Richardson scored a record twelve League hat-tricks for Albion – his first in November 1931 at West Ham (won 5-1); his last at home against Liverpool in February 1938 (also won 5-1).

Players from nine different nationalities have topped Albion's seasonal League scoring charts, among them Paul Peschisolido (Canada), Kanu (Nigeria), Diomansy Kamara (France/Senegal), Peter Odemwingie (Uzbekistan/Nigeria) and Romelu Lukaku (Belgium).